# THE Historical Jesus Through Catholic AND Jewish Eyes

# THE Historical Jesus Through Catholic AND Jewish Eyes

EDITED BY

Leonard J. Greenspoon
Dennis Hamm, S. J.
Bryan F. LeBeau

TRINITY PRESS INTERNATIONAL
Harrisburg, Pennsylvania

Trinity Press International
P.O. Box 1321, Harrisburg, PA 17105

*Trinity Press International is a division of the Morehouse Group.*

*Cover art:*    Detail showing head of Christ by Jan Gossaert,
               Museo del Prado, Madrid, Spain. Scala/Art Resource, N.Y.

*Cover design:*  Corey Kent

*Library of Congress Cataloging-in-Publication Data*
The historical Jesus through Catholic and Jewish eyes / edited by
Leonard Greenspoon, Dennis Hamm, and Bryan Le Beau.
     p. cm.
  Includes bibliographical references and index.
  ISBN 1-56338-322-5 (pbk. : alk. paper)
     1. Jesus Christ—Historicity. 2. Jesus Christ—Jewish interpretations.
  I. Le Beau, Bryan F. II. Greenspoon, Leonard J. (Leonard Jay)
  III. Hamm, M. Dennis.

BT303.2 .H49 2000
232.9'08—dc21                                          00-037413

Printed in the United States of America

00  01  02  03  04  05    10  9  8  7  6  5  4  3  2  1

To

Philip M. Klutznick (1907–1999)
Donor of Creighton University's Philip M. and Ethel Klutznick Chair
in Jewish Civilization

&

Michael G. Morrison, S. J.
President of Creighton University from 1981 to 2000

*For their leadership in bringing together the Omaha Jewish Community
and Creighton University, a Catholic and Jesuit University*

# CONTENTS

# PREFACE

"Who do people say that I am?" (Mark 8:27). Jesus confronted his disciples with this query at Caesarea Philippi. Their responses ("John the Baptist," "Elijah," "one of the prophets") on that occasion have been multiplied, myriad times in myriad contexts, as generations of scholars and believers have sought to articulate their own understandings of the "who-ness" of Jesus.

Time and place, in their practically infinite variety, have been among the most decisive factors in fashioning pictures of Jesus. The late 1990s, when we put together two "historical Jesus" colloquia, recorded an unusually rich array of answers—the stuff of magazine covers and television specials as much as sermons and retreats. For us place entails not only the American Midwest, where good sense and civility do indeed reign supreme, but the particulars of Creighton University—a Catholic, Jesuit comprehensive university with an active Center for the Study of Religion and Society—and its longstanding and warm relationship with Omaha's Jewish community—as encapsulated in the Philip M. and Ethel Klutznick Chair in Jewish Civilization. These two audiences, these two constituencies, provided decisive and positive focus for our colloquia, from planning to the events themselves to post-event evaluation. It is therefore fitting that we dedicate this volume to two individuals—Philip M. Klutznick and Michael G. Morrison, S. J.—whose joint legacy so fully embodies the "friendship among neighbors" that is "beautiful in the sight of God" (Sir 25:1).

# ACKNOWLEDGMENTS

It takes a small army of people to organize and execute two major colloquia and then to publish a volume of papers based on those colloquia and the subsequent contributions of other scholars. Such is the case here, and it is impossible to thank everyone by name. Nevertheless, we would like to acknowledge the contributions of the following people and organizations, without whom neither the colloquia nor this volume would have been possible.

We thank all of the authors who contributed such fine pieces to this collection on the historical Jesus. We are grateful to the planning committee that assisted in organizing the colloquia, including, other than the editors, Richard Hauser, S. J., Professor of Theology; Michael Lawler, the Amelia B. and Emil G. Graf Faculty Chair in Catholic Theology; Susan A. Calef, Assistant Professor of Theology; and David Schultenover, S. J., Professor of Theology—all of Creighton University.

We would like to express our appreciation to those people and organizations that supported the colloquia, either by their generous monetary contributions or services-in-kind: Creighton's Center for the Study of Religion and Society; Creighton's Dean of the College of Arts and Sciences, Michael Proterra, S. J.; the Nebraska Humanities Council; and the Jewish Federation of Omaha.

Finally, we would like to thank Trinity Press International's Editorial Director Henry Carrigan and Managing Editor Laura Hudson for the energy and professional care with which they saw this volume through to completion.

# INTRODUCTION

*Dennis Hamm, S. J.*

The making of books about the Jesus of history continues apace. Increasingly, any new volume on that topic must justify its place on an already crowded shelf. This collection of essays makes distinctive contributions to the ongoing conversation regarding the historical Jesus because the studies derive from a unique set of circumstances and approach their subject from distinctive points of view. The bulk of this volume derives from two colloquia on historical Jesus research, one by Catholic scholars (two exegetes and a systematician), the other by four Jewish scholars of Christian origins. These studies are complemented by two fresh reviews of the literature, one by a Jewish scholar and one by a Christian.

Three essays in this collection derive from the colloquium held in March 1997 at Creighton University entitled, "*Now* What Are They Saying about Jesus?" Sponsored by Creighton's Center for the Study of Religion and Society, the forum was created as a response to the growing interest, and media notoriety, generated by Robert Funk's Jesus Seminar. The impression left by some accounts of the Seminar's work was that the integrity and veracity of the Gospels were gradually dissolving under the scrutiny of a group of scholars casting votes with colored beads. Meanwhile, those of us who work professionally in biblical studies knew that the historical study of Jesus had been going on for more than a century and that the Jesus Seminar did not represent the consensus of contemporary New Testament scholarship. It seemed to the board of the Center that here, surely, was an issue calling for public analysis and clarification. To this end, we invited three prominent Catholic scholars—Luke Timothy Johnson, Daniel J. Harrington, S. J., and Monika K. Hellwig—to address various aspects of historical Jesus research.

The success of that colloquium inspired Leonard J. Greenspoon, holder of Creighton's Philip and Ethel Klutznick Chair in Jewish Civilization, Bryan F. Le Beau, then director of the Center for the Study of Religion and Society, and Dennis Hamm, S. J., professor in the department of theology, to put together a sequel, "Jesus and Christian Origins through Jewish Eyes." For this forum, held in March 1998, we invited four Jewish scholars known for their study of Jesus and early Christian writings—Michael J. Cook, Amy-Jill Levine, Adele Reinhartz, and Alan F. Segal. To our knowledge, this was the first conference devoted entirely to a consideration of these matters by eminent Jewish scholars. This colloquium, too, was enthusiastically received, not only by those attending, but also by the presenters themselves.

We realized that in these stimulating presentations we had the makings of a book. Since, however, they alluded to and presumed a knowledge of a history of historical Jesus research that is a good deal longer than its contemporary expression, we felt that readers of this collection would be well served by a fuller account of that research. Such reviews of historical Jesus research have been competently written by a number of scholars. Our survey surfaced a crisp review of the literature by Bernard Brandon Scott, "From Reimarus to Crossan: Stages in a Quest," *Currents in Research: Biblical Studies*, 2 (1994) 253–80. We asked Dr. Scott to update that survey for this volume. Further, to maintain the Christian/Jewish balance, we asked a young Jewish scholar, Jonathan D. Brumberg-Kraus, to sketch a review of the Jewish research on the Jesus of history. Finally, Dr. Greenspoon presents some reflections in an afterword.

Thus, we have here the products of two colloquia, Catholic and Jewish, complemented by two fuller reviews of the literature—one from a Christian perspective and one from a Jewish perspective—together with Dr. Greenspoon's final reflections. The ten essays make, we believe, a distinctive contribution to the present conversation about the Jesus of history.

Bernard Brandon Scott opens the volume by providing a historical framework in which to place the papers from the two Creighton historical

Jesus colloquia of 1997–98. He has updated his 1994 survey of the historical Jesus literature so that it covers the period from Reimarus and the late eighteenth century through the final years of the second millennium. Scott, Distinguished Professor of New Testament at the Phillips Theological Seminary of the University of Tulsa, has long been an active member of both the Society of Biblical Literature and the Catholic Biblical Association. His books include *Jesus, Symbol-Maker for the Kingdom* (1981), *Hear Then the Parable* (1989), *In Search of Wisdom* (1993), and *Hollywood Dreams and Biblical Stories* (1994).

Luke Timothy Johnson is Woodruff Professor of New Testament and Christian Origins at Emory University and author of a number of books, most recently, the Anchor commentary, *The Letter of James* (1995), a new edition of his *Writings of the New Testament* (1999), *The Real Jesus: The Misguided Quest for the Historical Jesus and the Truth of the Traditional Gospels* (1996), and *Living Jesus: Learning the Heart of the Gospel* (1999). Johnson addresses the question, "Are we still looking for the real Jesus?" He reviews the work of the Jesus Seminar, sees it as forcing an artificial choice between faith and scholarship, and he concludes that their quest is misguided on five counts.

Daniel J. Harrington, S. J., professor of New Testament at Weston School of Theology and editor of *New Testament Abstracts* and the Liturgical Press's Sacra Pagina series of biblical commentaries, is the author of some eighteen books including, recently, *The Maccabean Revolt: Anatomy of a Biblical Revolution* (1988), *John's Thought and Theology* (1990), *Wisdom Texts from Qumran* (1996), and *Who Is Jesus? Why Is He Important? An Invitation to the New Testament* (1999). In the present volume Harrington focuses on "Retrieving the Jewishness of Jesus: Recent Developments." He explores four recent developments that touch on the Jewishness of Jesus: (1) the relevance of the Dead Sea Scrolls to questions about New Testament language describing Jesus and the origin of the Christian movement, (2) the recognition of Jesus as Jewish wisdom teacher, (3) renewed discussion regarding who killed Jesus and why, and (4) the Jewish context of the Gospel of Matthew and why it is at once the most Jewish and the most anti-Jewish Gospel.

Monika K. Hellwig, a systematic theologian, has taught at Georgetown University since 1967, where she was the Landegger Distinguished Professor of Theology from 1990 to 1996. She currently serves as executive director of the Association of Catholic Colleges and Universities. She is a past president of the Catholic Theological Society of America (1986–87) and associate editor of the *Journal of Ecumenical Studies* (1973–present). Some of her recent books include *Jesus the Compassion of God* (1983), *The Eucharist and the Hunger of the World* (2nd ed., 1992), and *History, Context, and Implications of Feminist Theology* (published in Chinese, 1995). Her contribution to this volume, "Historical Jesus Research: Its Relevance to Thoughtful Christians and to Systematic Theologians," asserts the need for historical research into Jesus and the Gospels to overcome our own distortions and to steer a sober course between the polarities of fundamentalism on the one side and deconstruction on the other.

Michael J. Cook, an ordained rabbi, is the Sol and Arlene Bronstein Professor of Judaeo-Christian Studies at Cincinnati's Hebrew Union College–Jewish Institute of Religion. Cook teaches the only required course on New Testament at any rabbinical seminary in the United States. He has written *Evolving Jewish Views of Jesus* (1990), *Removing the Veil: Modern Jews and the New Testament* (forthcoming), and *The Role of Jews in the Trial of Jesus: Modern Scholarship vs. Modern Theater* (1994). To this volume, Cook contributes "Jewish Reflections on Jesus: Some Abiding Trends." After sketching the orientations he finds characteristic of most Jewish readers of Christian material, he outlines and discusses five characteristically Jewish approaches to processing Gospel presentations of Jesus, especially regarding the paradox of the Jewish Jesus implicitly expressing anti-Jewish theology.

Amy-Jill Levine presently serves as E. Rhodes and Leona B. Carpenter Professor of New Testament Studies at Vanderbilt University's School of Divinity. One of only a handful of Jewish scholars holding such a chair in a Christian school of divinity, she has written extensively on the Gospels and on women both as biblical characters and as biblical scholars. Levine's books include *The Social and Ethnic Dimensions of Matthean Salvation History: "Go Nowhere among the Gentiles"* (1988), *Threatened Bodies: Women, Culture, Apocrypha* (forthcoming), and *"Women Like This": New Perspectives on Jewish Women in the Greco-Roman World* (1991). Her contribution to this volume is "Jesus, Divorce, and Sexuality: A Jewish Critique." Dr. Levine's fresh probing of Jesus' sayings on marriage and divorce provides a striking example of the difference the social location of a scholar can make. The fact that Levine is a Jewish woman entitles her to be appropriately defensive regarding sweeping characterizations of early first-century Jewish society. She discerns that many Christian generalizations about Jewish life contemporary with Jesus are greatly influenced by the desire of Christian scholars to describe that social life in a way that acts as a foil to the positive aspects they wish to affirm about Jesus.

Adele Reinhartz is professor of biblical studies in the Department of Religious Studies at McMaster University and associate dean of McMaster's School of Graduate Studies. She presently serves as president of the Canadian Society of Biblical Studies, and regularly participates in interfaith activities. Her writings include *Befriending the Beloved Disciple: A Jewish Reading of the Gospel of John* (2001), *"Why Ask My Name?" Anonymity and Identity in Biblical Narrative* (1998), and *The Word in the World* (1993). Her contribution to this volume is "Jesus of Hollywood: A Jewish Perspective." Reinhartz's project is to assess cinematic portraits of Jesus' Jewishness from her point of view as a Jewish New Testament scholar. She identifies various streams of Jesus scholarship reflected in the Jesus films of Zeffirelli, Scorcese, Pasolini, and Arcand. She pays particular attention to the portrayal of the role of Jews in bringing about the death of Jesus. She also reviews how filmmakers use the Jesus material to imply analogies with contemporary issues. Finally, Reinhartz declares which are her favorite Jesus films and why.

Alan F. Segal is the Ingeborg Professor of Jewish Studies at Barnard College, Columbia University. Increasingly popular as a Jewish scholar of Christian origins, his books include *The Other Judaisms of Late Antiquity* (1987), *Paul the Convert: The Apostasy and Apostolate of Saul of Tarsus* (1990), and *Rebecca's Children: Judaism and Christianity in the Roman World* (1986). His contribution to this collection is "Jesus in the Eyes of One Jewish Scholar." He notes that the "criterion of dissimilarity," while leaving enough to guarantee the existence of Jesus, necessarily delivers to the historian a totally non-Jewish Jesus. He is convinced that Jesus lived and died for his Judaism, that he was an apocalypticist, and that his followers saw his death as a martyrdom and experienced his continued presence as resurrected messiah and the Son of man of Daniel 7. The main thrust of Segal's paper is to describe how Jesus' apocalypticism is similar to, and different from, the community that wrote the Dead Sea scrolls.

Jonathan D. Brumberg-Kraus, a young Ph.D. in New Testament with a minor in rabbinics, now teaching at Wheaton College (Norton, Mass.), has focused most of his research and writing on eating rituals and the interface between Jewish tradition and the Last Supper of Jesus. Along with several articles in this area, he has written *Meals, Ritual, and the Textual Construction of Meaning: Christian and Jewish Transformations of Hellenistic Symposium Literature* (2000). For this volume, Jonathan has supplied a review of Jesus research in Jewish scholarship, "Jesus as Other People's Scripture." Writing from the viewpoint of his own involvement as a Jewish scholar of Christian scriptures, he shows how American Jewish scholarship on Jesus has moved from focusing on the "Jewish" Jesus of history over the "Christian" Christ of faith, to the study of how Jesus functions as religious authority for Christians. It is a move from the historical personality of Jesus to Jesus' religious meaning as embedded in Christian texts. Finally, Brumberg-Kraus explores what the study of Jesus precisely as "other people's scripture" has meant and can mean especially for contemporary American Jews.

Leonard J. Greenspoon concludes the volume with his reflections on the two colloquia that produced these essays and the dialogue they engendered between Catholics and Jews on the historical Jesus.

# 1. NEW OPTIONS IN AN OLD QUEST

*Bernard Brandon Scott*

Recent scholarship has evidenced a renewed interest in and, more important, confidence about our historical knowledge of Jesus. Marcus Borg has referred to "a renaissance in Jesus studies"; N. T. Wright has called it a third quest, and James Charlesworth has written of "a renewed study of the Jesus of history." E. P. Sanders reflects the renewed confidence of many scholars: "The dominant view today seems to be that we can know pretty well what Jesus was out to accomplish, that we can know a lot about what he said, and that those two things make sense within the world of first-century Judaism."[1]

Before beginning an essay of this scope, a caveat is in order. The vast bibliography generated by this topic just in the past ten years cannot be dealt with in the space allotted. I hope to represent fairly the positions of the various scholars without engaging in caricature. Oversimplification goes with the task and the reader should bear that in mind. I am trying in this essay to provide the reader with a tracking of the important options that have shaped research and debate. The sketch follows for the most part the chronology of the question but at the same time is critically systematic.

## Stage One: The Life of Jesus

In *The Quest of the Historical Jesus*, Albert Schweitzer pointed to "the critical investigation of the life of Jesus" as "the greatest achievement of German theology." The English title of his book, apparently the brilliant suggestion of its translator, W. Montgomery, has served as the title for the whole enterprise. Schweitzer also noted that this course of research "has laid down the conditions and determined the course of the religious thinking of the future." That prophecy has yet to come true, although it may yet.[2]

Despite Schweitzer's prophecy, the relation between the quest of the historical Jesus and Christian faith has been problematic from the beginning. The origins of New Testament critical scholarship lie in the project started by Herman Samuel Reimarus (1694–1768). His research, unpublished in his lifetime because he feared public reaction, had as its goal the demonstration that Christianity was a fraud because it was based on a lie. In Reimarus's reconstruction Jesus' disciples stole the body.[3] Reimarus's work was published by Gothold Lessing (1729–1781), who also prepared a response to it, not with the intent of proving Christian faith, but of showing how Christianity's essence was likewise the essence of deism. "Accidental truths of history can never become the proof of necessary truths of reason."[4] For both Lessing and Reimarus historical research was at odds with Christian faith.

One of the long-term results of the revolution begun by the printing press was a bifurcation in attitudes towards the Bible. On the one hand, mass production of the Bible in the vernacular made its meaning seem transparent to the contemporary reader. The distance between reader and Bible was foreshortened until it was almost eliminated. The eventual outcome was literalism, fundamentalism, rendering the Bible's meaning transparent. On the other hand, the printing press and early printers developed the very scholarship that so antagonized the literalists. The need of printers for translations in turn demanded dictionaries, better texts, parallels, and other tools of scholarship. A clash was inevitable.[5] Between Gutenberg's invention (1455) and the publication of Reimarus's *Fragments* in 1774 was the intellectual ferment of the Enlightenment. Thus, the quest is a direct result of cultural shifts brought on by the printing press and the Enlightenment. There is not only a theological interest in Jesus, but also an historical and cultural one.

Schweitzer's summary of the quest in the eighteenth and nineteenth centuries narrated their futility. Inevitably, in Schweitzer's famous image, the reflection at the bottom of the well was that of the historian, not Jesus. For example, David Friedrich Strauss, in his massive *Das Leben Jesu*, sought to demonstrate the mythological character of the gospels. While this life of Jesus was the negative, critical part of his program, the positive was essentially a Hegelian substitution.[6] Even Schweitzer's own program had an anti-Christian edge. Although he sought to discredit the liberal lives of Jesus, his apocalyptic messiah was unfit as a basis for traditional Christian faith.[7] Hans Conzelmann summarized this aspect of the quest in the first sentence of an article on Jesus: "The historical and substantive presupposition for modern research into the life of Jesus is emancipation from the traditional christological dogma on the basis of the principle of reason."[8]

A search for a firm foundation on which to build has been an essential mark of the quest in all its stages. Since the first stage sought a biography of Jesus, solving the synoptic problem began with Lessing. Markan priority, which argued that Mark's Gospel was the earliest and that the other gospels were dependent on it, seemed to offer a firm foundation on which to construct a biography of Jesus. Furthermore, unlike Matthew and Luke, Mark did not have embarrassing birth narratives or resurrection appearances. What brought to a halt this quest to write a biography was Wilhelm Wrede's *Messianic Secret* (1901), in which he argued that Jesus' silencing of his identity as the Messiah was a Markan strategy to account for the fact that the confession of Jesus as the Messiah actually resulted from post-Easter Christian confession. Thus, the plot of the first Gospel was Mark's, not a product of historical memory.[9] If the plot of the first Gospel was a product of imagination and not memory, then no reliable basis for a biography of Jesus existed. The sequence of events will be forever a mystery.

The demonstration of the impossibility of a biography of Jesus is a permanent achievement of this first stage of the quest and was further reinforced by two important works of the post World War I era. K. L. Schmidt, in his *Der Rahmen Geschichte Jesu* (*The Outline of the History of Jesus*), demonstrated that the connecting links between the individual units (pericopes) of Mark's Gospel were the product of the author.[10] So the author was responsible for both the plot (messianic secret) and outline. Finally, the development of form criticism in the 1920s highlighted the creative powers of early Christian communities and the importance of their situation (*Sitz im Leben*) in the development of the oral tradition.[11] Form criticism reduced still more the ability to write a life of Jesus by questioning the tradition's reliability on the basis of the creative power of oral tradition.

Martin Kähler crafted the most important theological response to the first quest and the title of his book summarizes his program: *The So-called Historical Jesus and the Historic, Biblical Christ.*[12] Since historical criticism could not deliver the assured and certain results that faith required, Kähler built a wall of separation between Jesus as reconstructed by the historians and the Christ of faith to which the Bible witnessed. This wall pronounced the historical Jesus irrelevant to Christian faith and thus diminished interest in such research. In Bultmann's famous statement, "The message of Jesus is a presupposition for the theology of the New Testament."[13] The quest went to sleep for a while.

A permanent gain of the first stage was the rejection of the effort to write a biography of Jesus. We do not and never will have materials for a real biography of Jesus.

## Stage Two: The Message

The quest in Germany flared up under the aegis of the "New Quest" of the historical Jesus.[14] The New Quest was allied with the new hermeneutics, both products of the Bultmann school, a group of German and American scholars in the period after World War II.[15] The New Quest sought to overcome Kähler's gaping abyss by attacking the implicit docetism in the separation of the Jesus of history from the Christ of faith by stressing as a historical concern the identification of the crucified and risen Lord. In a seminal essay, Ernst Käsemann wrote, "The question of the historical Jesus is, in its legitimate form, the question of the continuity of the times and within the variation of the kerygma." The gospel, which exposes an existential understanding of being, unifies the historical Jesus and the preaching of the church. "[T]he real history of Jesus is always happening afresh; it is now the history of the exalted Lord, but it does not cease to be the earthly history it once was, in which the call and claim of the Gospel are encountered."[16] As Leander Keck has pointed out, the New Quest was only following clues already planted by Bultmann.[17] Even though the New

Quest was mostly a German Protestant enterprise, the most significant study of Jesus' message produced under the influence of the New Quest was by a Roman Catholic Dutch theologian, Edward Schillebeeckx, *Jesus: An Experiment in Christology.*[18]

The interest in the kergyma led to the New Quest's distinctive interest in Jesus' message and his sayings. In the previous generation, form criticism had successfully isolated these sayings. Just as the first stage sought to secure a sure foundation for a life of Jesus, this second stage tried to lay a foundation by authenticating the sayings of Jesus. Norman Perrin, in *Rediscovering the Teaching of Jesus*, produced the most influential examination of criteria. His formulation of the criterion of dissimilarity has become classic: "The earliest form of a saying we can reach may be regarded as authentic if it can be shown to be dissimilar to characteristic emphases both of ancient Judaism and of the early Church."[19] This criterion was for Perrin the strongest one and produced the most characteristic message of Jesus.[20] Thus, what was distinctive about Jesus "will be found not in the things which he shares with his contemporaries, but in the things wherein he differs from them." [21]

The New Quest had a built-in contradiction at its heart. It relied on the criterion of dissimilarity to establish its sure foundation and to overcome what it saw as the docetic division created by Kähler's split between Jesus and the Christ. Yet the criterion of dissimilarity demanded a separation between Jesus and Christ, and between Jesus and Judaism.

While form critics were not interested in the quest, Joachim Jeremias's studies, built on their results, provided an extremely important bridge to the third stage of the quest. First published in German in 1947 and translated into English in 1954, his *Die Gleichnis Jesu* went through eight editions, with three revisions in English. Jeremias rejected Kähler's position and claimed historical method for the service of Christian faith. For him, the parables were "the original rock of tradition," and he sought to "arrive at the earliest attainable form of Jesus' parabolic teaching" because "[o]nly the Son of Man and his word can invest our message with full authority." For Jeremias, the quest is not something to fear as antagonistic to Christian faith; it is a kind of sacrament that

6 · Bernard Brandon Scott

makes Jesus present. "We stand right before Jesus when reading his parables."[22] This common sense basis, devoid of the arcane German distinction between *historisch* ("historical") and *geschichtlich* ("historic"), appealed to the common sense tradition of both Great Britain and the United States.

The trajectory of scholarship represented by Jeremias, extending back to Adolf Jülicher through C. H. Dodd, was continued in the United States by Robert Funk, Dan O. Via Jr., John Dominic Crossan, and the present author.[23] Jeremias had pursued a form of critical analysis along historical lines that sought to reconstruct the Aramaic *ipsissima verba* ("actual words") of Jesus. Funk and Via introduced the concerns of American New Criticism and literary theory into the debate. They were able to move beyond the old quest by introducing new methods that raised new hermeneutical concerns. Even though at times highly indebted to German scholarship, both set the quest on indigenous American grounds. This American line of parable study gradually arrived at a consensus of Jesus the teacher of subversive wisdom that has underlain much of the quest's third stage.

Jeremias's English student, Perrin, who taught at the University of Chicago, pursued a second line of development. In a series of studies, Perrin explored the kingdom of God.[24] Perrin employed the methods of literary theory and especially the understanding of symbol developed by Philip Wheelright to redefine kingdom as a symbol,[25] rather than as a concept whose meaning could be determined by historical analysis.[26] This called into question the understanding of the kingdom of God, dominant since Johannes Weiss and Schweitzer, as an apocalyptic cipher for the literal end of the world.[27] Perrin advanced this argument by calling into question the apocalyptic assumption. Even though he was a student of Jeremias, he was closer to Dodd's realized eschatology. Conflict over the timetable of the kingdom and its lack of resolution is a defining marker of the third stage.

### The Third Stage: The Jewish Jesus

Jeremias and the tradition that followed in his wake had taken the study of Jesus' message as far as it could go. Unlike the quest's first stage, the second one did not so much reach bankruptcy as a dead end. A new stage demanded progress in three areas: (1) new data was needed to overcome the interpretive impasses; (2) new methods were needed, not only because historical methods had failed to provide a sure foundation, but also because the social sciences were penetrating New Testament scholarship; and (3) new models were needed to understand Jesus. Jesus the preacher had been exhausted.

Clearly the quest now is at a new stage that attempts to meet these three challenges in various ways. What best typifies this third stage is an effort to understand, first, Jesus as a Jew within the context of the diversification of second temple Judaism and, second, the forces that generated the plurality of the pre-Constantine Jesus tradition. If stage one sought a biography and stage two tried to isolate Jesus' message, the third stage seeks a synchronic Jesus, enmeshed in the systems of both Judaism and early Christianity.

## Charismatic Hasid

In the 1970s important studies by Geza Vermes and Morton Smith jump-started the third stage because they provided both new models and new data outside the sayings tradition. The title of Vermes's book denotes the twin thrust of his work: *Jesus the Jew, A Historian's Reading of the Gospels.*[28] Vermes, typical of third questers, acts as a historian and is not timid about history's abilities. Since Vermes is a Jew, he does not approach the quest from a Christian perspective. For him Jesus is a Jew, not a Jew who founds Christianity. In itself this is not surprising, except one should remember that the use of the criterion of dissimilarity had led to an image of Jesus in which "he cannot be integrated into the background of the Jewish piety of his time."[29]

Vermes attacks both poles of the criterion of dissimilarity. He takes the evidence the gospels present about Jesus, thus accepting continuity with the early community, and then attempts to explain that evidence on the basis of Galilean Judaism, thereby making Jesus intelligible within Judaism. "The Synoptists are unanimous in presenting him as an exorcist, healer and teacher. They also emphasize that the deepest impression made by Jesus on his contemporaries resulted from his mastery over devils and disease, and the magnetic power of his preaching."[30] The New Quest had dealt more with the "meaning" of Jesus' teaching, whereas Vermes emphasizes the "power." Furthermore, the New Quest had virtually ignored the exorcisms and healings,[31] whereas Vermes puts them at the center. For him, Jesus is an example of the Galilean holy man in charismatic Judaism. He is a product, not of rabbinic, but of common Judaism, from the villages.

Jesus exemplifies the miracle-working holy man, a well-established pattern in Judaism. "The pattern set by the miracle-working prophets Elijah and Elisha was first of all applied by postbiblical tradition to other saints of the scriptural past; they, too, were credited with powers of healing and exorcism deriving not from incantations and drugs or the observance of elaborate rubrics, but solely from speech and touch."[32] Jesus fits in with Honi the Circle-Drawer (circa first century B.C.E.), mentioned in both rabbinic texts and Josephus, and Hanina ben Dosa (prior to 70 C.E.). Both were well known for their ability to influence God through prayer. A single story referred to by Vermes can stand for this charismatic tradition of the holy man:

> When Rabbi Hanina ben Dosa prayed, a poisonous reptile bit him, but he did not interrupt his prayer. They [the onlookers] departed and found the same "snake" dead at the opening of its hole. "Woe to the man," they exclaimed, "bitten by a snake, but woe to the snake which has bitten Rabbi Hanina ben Dosa."[33]

Vermes himself has found that "the chief finding of Jesus the Jew is the recognition of Jesus within the earliest Gospel tradition, prior to Christian theological speculation, as a charismatic prophetic preacher and miracle worker, the outstanding 'Galilean Hasid.'"[34] This chief finding, Vermes's contribution to the quest, is hard to overestimate because it has changed the options. Whereas the New Quest had put the theological question at the center in reaction to Kähler, Vermes sets aside the theological issue. He is neither for nor against Christian claims on behalf of Jesus. They are irrelevant to his historical portrait of Jesus the Jew. More important, he demonstrates that Jesus did make sense within the context of first-century Judaism situated within the

Hasid tradition, a popular rather than elite tradition. The full significance of this social location will only become evident with the addition
of the social sciences to the historian's toolbox.

The downside of Vermes's study is that, in the end, he overlooks or
ignores the genuine accomplishments of the form critics. In his effort
to take the Gospels seriously, he tends at times to take them too much
at face value. Too much is explained by his model of charismatic
Judaism, and he does not sufficiently allow for development or dependence within the Gospel tradition.

### The Magician

Morton Smith's *Jesus the Magician* has not had the influence of
Vermes' work, probably because it has a more threatening edge to
Christian theology. In that sense, Smith's work belongs in the tradition
of Reimarus and is reminiscent of that earlier program. He sees Jesus as
a magician emerging from the syncretistic environment of Galilee. At
Jesus' baptism he receives a magic spirit and becomes a (son of) God,
then studies magic in Egypt and gives enchanted food to his followers.[35]
Under Paul's influence the heretical sect founded by Jesus swings back
toward more conventional religious practices, and the Gospel writers
began to cover up the clues. But Smith, with the help of the Egyptian
magical papyri and Jewish magical books, claims to have correctly fer-
reted out the remaining clues. Like Reimarus, Smith claims Christianity
was founded on a deceit.

If this were the extent of Smith's book, one might be tempted to dismiss it as bias. But Smith was a serious scholar, and his discovery of
Secret Mark is a major, though controversial, contribution to New
Testament studies.[36] His study of Jesus as magician makes an important
contribution and represents both the strengths and weaknesses of the
quest's third stage.

In comparison with Vermes, who views the miracle-working activity
within the confines of charismatic Judaism, Smith views both Judaism
and Christianity within the context of the Roman Empire. This difference between Vermes and Smith represents an important shift in some
of the third stage studies. To borrow an analogy from science, the world

looks different through a microscope (close view), or seen from earth (middle view), or from space (long view). A similar problem exists here. The New Quest took a close view, Vermes a middle one, and Smith a long one. At a close level, differentiation stands out; at a middle level, Jesus the Jew appears; and from a long view, Judaism, Jesus, and early Christianity find their context in the swirling currents of the Roman Empire.

Like Vermes, Smith departs from the tracks laid down by the New Quest by starting with the miracle tradition. The miracle worker model accounts for the details of Jesus' life.

> A man who can do miracles is thought to have some sort of supernatural power ... [H]is power is thought holy ... [H]is sayings and actions will be remembered. ... If his followers begin to think him the Messiah, and if they become so numerous and enthusiastic as to frighten the civil authorities, he will soon be in serious trouble. Thus the rest of the tradition about Jesus can be understood if we begin with the miracles.

Beginning with the miracles soon produces an explanation of the rise of early Christianity. On the other hand, Smith argues that the miracles remain unintelligible if one begins with the sayings. In the rabbinic tradition, which is almost devoid of miracles, teachers of the Torah were not "made over into miracle workers." The same is true for apocalyptic sayers. A miracle worker, however, could easily come to be thought a prophet and an authority on the Law." Therefore, these other understandings of Jesus are later developments from this one model of the miracle worker.[37]

Smith draws heavily on the parallels with Apollonius of Tyana, a contemporary of Jesus whom Philostratus portrays more as a philosopher than a miracle worker.[38] Smith analyzes not only the parallels between Jesus and Apollonius, but also the attacks on the two. In Jesus' case, Smith takes Celsus's attack on Christianity as representing not just the opposition to Christianity in the last half of the second century, but also an earlier Jewish attack on Jesus. For example, since both a late rabbinic story and Celsus report that Jesus studied magic in Egypt, Smith argues that this story goes back to Jesus' historical opponents and that

Matthew's story of a flight to Egypt attempts to cover it up. There are
many problems with this proposal, not the least of which is that Celsus
must be reconstructed from Origen's comments and the rabbinic text is
late and less than sure. So one should take Smith's argument as very
tendentious. Nevertheless, this type of argument is important if used
more selectively. There is nothing improbable about Jewish propaganda
against early Christianity. There certainly was Christian propaganda
against Judaism, as the Gospels indicate.

Smith makes a strong case for the centrality of the miracle tradition
in understanding the historical Jesus. While magic is a pejorative term
and Smith opts for an outsider's view of Jesus as the correct one, nevertheless magic and the miraculous were widespread and fundamental
in the ancient world, and the distinction between the two is often a
matter of taste.[39] In a very intriguing study of Jesus' miraculous activity, A. E. Harvey remarks on its notable ambiguity. The exorcisms
would clearly leave Jesus open to charges of sorcery. Harvey concludes
that this ambiguity on the part of Jesus was deliberate. Furthermore, he
sees the synoptic recounting of the miracle tradition as unlike other
comparable Hellenistic parallels in its attitude. "They [the Gospels] do
not exaggerate the miracle or add sensational details, like the authors of
early Christian hagiography; but nor do they show the kind of detachment, amounting at times to scepticism, which is found in Herodotus
or Lucian and even to a certain extent in Philostratus."[40]

In the end, it is not Smith's anti-Christian bias that undoes him.
Such a bias is no more problematic than the counterbias of Christian
scholars. It falls to the scholarly discipline to filter out the bias of individual scholars. More problematic is the totalizing aspect of his model
and the lumping together without discrimination the various Gospel
portraits to construct an outline of Jesus' life. The positive gains of the
earlier scholarship just cannot be set aside to fit a totalizing theory.

**Restorer of the Temple**

E. P. Sanders's *Jesus and Judaism* should probably be noted as the first
full-scale study of the quest's third stage. Sanders came to this study as
an established student of Judaism and a major scholar on Paul.[41] He

takes a middle view, positioning Jesus within the context of second temple Judaism and, even though he sees as the key issue the explanation of the death of Jesus, the Roman Empire seldom comes into view. The cause of the death of Jesus is not Rome, but Jewish (Sadducean) authorities.

The search for a sure foundation has marked the quest in each stage, always threatened by the very nature of the material available for investigation. Sanders sets out in advance what is required of a good hypothesis to explain the historical Jesus. First, "it should situate Jesus believably in Judaism and yet explain why the movement initiated by him eventually broke with Judaism." Characteristic of the third stage, Jesus is a Jew and must make sense as a Jew. But at the same time the seeds for the eventual break between Christianity and Judaism should be found in Jesus and not just in the early community. The second important aspect of a good hypothesis is that "it should offer a connection between his activity and his death." There are four interrelated elements in Sanders's reconstruction: (1) "what Jesus had in mind," (2) "how he saw his relationship to his nation," (3) "the reason for his death," and (4) "the beginning of the Christian movement."[42]

Sanders rejects the sayings tradition as a firm foundation for two reasons. First, he does not believe that there exists a consensus among scholars "on the authenticity of the sayings material, either in whole or in part." Second, starting with the sayings leads to the assumption that Jesus was a teacher. In Sanders's judgment one cannot satisfactorily account for "the conclusion and aftermath of his career" with such a starting point, because people are not put to death for words but deeds. "[T]he teaching material in the Gospels has not yielded a convincing historical depiction of Jesus—one which sets him firmly in Jewish history, which explains his execution, and which explains why his followers formed a persecuted messianic sect."[43]

Having rejected the sayings tradition as a sure foundation on which to build his hypothesis, Sanders posits what he takes to be an indubitable foundation stone. For Sanders "the principal context" of Jesus' work is Jewish eschatology: "[T]he line from John the Baptist to Paul and the other early apostles is the line of Jewish eschatology and it would be misleading to move the centre of our investigation off that line." This assumption is absolutely essential to Sanders's sure foundation, and the line from John the Baptist to Jesus to Paul can be considered the canonical line. The second element in Sanders's sure foundation is a list of eight facts he considers beyond doubt about Jesus, out of which he selects "Jesus engaged in a controversy about the temple" as the best sure fact on which to begin because of its interconnection with the death of Jesus. Sanders's confidence is high: Jesus' temple controversy "offers almost as good an entry for the study of Jesus and his relationship to his contemporaries as would a truly eyewitness account of the trial."[44]

Having set a firm foundation, Sanders must admit "that the question of Jesus and the temple brings with it the amount of uncertainty which is usual in the study of the Gospels." First, he must oppose the opinion that what Jesus was about was cleansing the temple. "Those who write about Jesus' desire to return the temple to its 'original,' 'true' purpose, the 'pure' worship of God, seem to forget that the principal function of any temple is to serve as a place for sacrifice, and that sacrifices require the supply of suitable animals." Yet the interpretation of the temple act as a cleansing goes back at least as far as Mark (11:17). For Sanders, Jesus' temple act "symbolized destruction."

> We should suppose that Jesus knew what he was doing: Like others, he regarded the sacrifices as commanded by God, he knew that they required a certain amount of trade, and he knew that making a gesture towards disrupting the trade represented an attack on the divinely ordained sacrifices. Thus I take it that the action at the very least symbolized an attack, and note that "attack" is not far from "destruction."[45]

Sanders bases his argument not only on the inner logic of his argument but also on what he takes as an "accurate memory of the principal point on which Jesus offended many of his contemporaries," namely, the threat to destroy the temple and in three days to rebuild it.[46] Ironically, the Gospels specifically refer to this as a false witness.

Sanders's reconstruction of Jewish eschatology provides the interpretative lock in his building block. "'Jewish eschatology' and 'the restoration of Israel' are almost synonymous," and a primary element in the restoration of Israel is the restoration of the temple. "The kingdom was at hand, and one of the things which that meant was that the old temple would be replaced by a new one," Sanders explains, even though he knows that the evidence on Jewish eschatology is neither that conclusive nor universal.[47] Yet this version of restoration eschatology, in his judgment, makes the best sense of Jesus' association with John the Baptist, his temple action and the aftermath it provoked, the resurrection, the belief of his disciples in his messiahship, and the gentile mission.

Sanders's proposal has provoked a lively debate. Jacob Neusner agrees with Sanders that Jesus' temple act was a symbolic action, but for him it was symbolic for the disciples, not the crowds. Jesus was trying to demonstrate to his disciples that the temple sacrifices should be replaced by the Eucharist, the tables of the money changers should be exchanged for tables of the Eucharist.[48] Neusner's proposal has not gained wide support because it is hard to understand why the Christian Gospels would not reflect such a meaning if such were the original. Craig Evans faces Sanders's proposal even more directly. "It seems to me that the tendency of the tradition would be exactly the opposite of what Sanders has proposed. Had Jesus' action indeed been designed to signify the temple's impending doom, we should expect that the evangelist Mark, if no one else, would have interpreted his actions as portending exactly that meaning."[49] Why then if Jesus' action originally involved the destruction of the temple, would the evangelists in a post-70 C.E. situation, after the actual destruction of the temple, picture it as a cleansing? Furthermore, a cleansing motif is plausible in Jesus' historical context. The ruling priests were viewed as corrupt and the Essenes were a group who viewed the temple as in need of cleansing. Evans also rejects Sanders's reconstruction of eschatology:

> "[T]here is no evidence whatsoever that a messiah or prophet or other eschatological figure was expected to destroy the Temple as a necessary prelude to building a new one. The evidence that a messiah was expected to build a new Temple is itself poorly attested (especially for the pre-70 C.E. period), never mind build

a new one when the old one was still standing, indeed was undergoing extensive remodeling.[50]

Others have gone even further. Bruce Chilton, while agreeing with Evans's critique of Sanders, has argued for a Pharisaic background to explain the temple action: "It was an occupation designed to prevent the sacrifice of animals acquired on the site, in trading that involved commerce within the Temple and obscured the Pharisaic understanding that such animals were to be fully the property of Israel (as distinct from the priesthood or the Temple)."[51] While Chilton's proposal is very suggestive, its main problem is that he makes Jesus over into a Pharisee. The placement of Jesus by Vermes and Smith in the common and not the elite tradition remains convincing.

George Wesley Buchanan and David Seeley have attacked the authenticity of the temple action itself. Buchanan attacks its historical probability as described in the Gospels.

> Would military policemen, without reacting, allow a man or group of men to come into this strategic, defended area and start an upheaval which involved driving people out of the building and overturning the furniture? . . . With the long history of conflict associated with feasts at Jerusalem against which Rome was well prepared, how could Jesus have been allowed to have walked away unmolested after this turmoil had taken place (Mark 11.19)?[52]

Seeley attacks the authenticity by forcibly arguing that Mark created the incident and that it fits his schema of blaming Judaism for the death of Jesus. If Mark composed the incident, why present it as a cleansing rather than a destruction?

> To suggest that the Messiah and the temple represented mutually exclusive modes of salvation would simply not make sense to any of Mark's readers familiar with Jewish thought. This would be especially true if those readers were still feeling the grief and shock which many must have experienced in the wake of the temple's destruction. . . . He had to insinuate smoothly and relatively unobtrusively the notion that Jesus' coming means the temple's end.[53]

Buchanan and Seeley clearly demonstrate that one cannot assume the historicity of the temple incident and that good evidence calls it into question. However, as Robert Miller has pointed out, even if Mark fails as historical, Thomas 71 keeps the issue alive.[54] How one evaluates that evidence depends on one's judgment about the dependence of Thomas on the synoptics.

The power of Sanders's reconstruction is also its weakness. He has taken an apparently simple and what he thought was an incontestable fact, Jesus' temple activity, and used it as a starting point from which to weave out in ever enlarging circles a whole cloth. Yet the lively debate that has surrounded Sanders's proposal only indicates that a sure foundation, a fortress beyond attack, is not to be found.

Sanders has continued the tendency of the third stage of placing the deeds in the forefront. Even more, he has raised in a forceful form the question of eschatology, a topic at the center of neither Vermes's nor Smith's analyses. Sanders sets out an imminent apocalyptic eschatology reminiscent of Schweitzer's view. Chilton among others has noted the irony of Sanders's position. Sanders disdains the sayings in favor of the deeds "and then proceeds to use an explicitly dogmatic context in order to interpret those deeds." Chilton accuses Sanders of the same anachronism as Schweitzer, of using later apocalyptic documents to "comprehend the motivation of Jesus."[55]

There is also a curious anomaly in Sanders's reconstruction. He sets the temple event at the center of Jesus' activity and portrays an imminent coming of the kingdom to destroy the old temple and rebuild a new one. Yet he insists that Jesus was apolitical.[56] It is hard to see how a deed as provocative as the temple action and the preaching of a *basileia* (empire, kingdom) can be apolitical.

The failure of Sanders's project demonstrates the problem with a method that is simply historical. Sanders's historical methodology has a traditional, almost positivistic cast as evidenced by his disdain for the sayings tradition. Literary criticism and the social sciences make no appearance. Documents are investigated in an almost Holmesian fashion. But is it so clear that history is so deterministic and lockstep? In the Roman Empire, justice was so marginal that one does not need much of an explanation for the death of a Galilean peasant.

In 1993 Sanders published *The Historical Figure of Jesus*. While this book lacks for the most part the scholarly apparatus of footnotes, it is not a simplified version of the earlier book, but a major reconsideration of his case for Jesus as a radical eschatologist. Since the publication of *Jesus and Judaism*, the third stage of the quest was now well underway. Sanders learned from the debate, so his second work is a good marker of fundamental fault lines in the quest.

Sanders has abandoned his eight so-called indisputable facts.[57] These proved more controversial than he probably anticipated. This points out how problematic and elusive is the search for a sure foundation.

For Sanders the linchpin is Jesus' eschatological program and its strongest support is what he takes to be the unbreakable line between John, Jesus, and Paul. This argument is a key marker of a major fault line in the third quest, so one should pay close attention to it. Sanders makes this argument even more explicit in *The Historical Figure of Jesus*. I will condense his argument:

John really did baptize Jesus. This, in turn, implies that Jesus agreed with John's message: it was time to repent in view of the coming wrath and *redemption*. . . .

Paul fiercely disputed some points with other Christians, but not this one. They all believed that Jesus would establish a kingdom in the very near future, in their lifetimes. . . .

At the beginning of Jesus' career, then we find him accepting the mission of John the Baptist, who said that the climax of history was at hand. Within no more than a decade after Jesus' execution, we have firm proof that his followers expected this dramatic event very soon. *Jesus must fit this context*. . . . This context is historically crucial, since it is the framework of Jesus' overall mission: it includes the man who baptized him, and also his own followers.[58]

Sanders thus maintains that without exception all early Christians accepted the apocalyptic worldview.[59] It should come as no surprise that Q The Synoptic Sayings Source is never mentioned in *The Historical Figure of Jesus*. In *Studying the Synoptic Gospels* (with Margaret Davies), he opts for a complicated solution to the synoptic problem that basically eliminates Q. Sanders and Davies refer to "believers in Q." "Now a few scholars are again attempting to define Q as a document: it really existed, it directly reflects *the* theology of *a* community. . . . This work is mostly of curiosity value, since it shows how far a hypothesis can be pushed despite its lack of fundamental support."[60] Of course, with the dismissal of Q and the insistence that all early Christians are apocalyptic in orientation, the wisdom tradition is not only set aside, but its existence is denied. Sanders does admit that the Gospel of Thomas is an early gospel, although he does not say how early: "Of all the apocryphal material, only some of the sayings in the Gospel of Thomas are worth consideration."[61] He never identifies these sayings and, aside from this reference to the Gospel of Thomas, Sanders makes no other mention of it.

Three key issues emerge here that define the debate. First, what I have termed the canonical line of John the Baptist, Jesus, and Paul form an axis for the apocalyptic interpretation of Jesus. Second, there is the status of Q. Does it exist and does it represent an early community and maybe the earliest witness to Jesus? And, finally, is the Gospel of Thomas independent of the synoptic Gospels? How one answers these three issues has become determinative for the picture of Jesus that emerges in the third quest.

### A Spirit-Filled Jesus

In *Jesus, A New Vision*, Marcus Borg attempts to avoid the historical constraints that plagued Sanders's proposal. He does not seek to confine Jesus to a single model but sees Jesus as "a charismatic who was a healer, sage, prophet, and revitalization movement founder."[62] He also rejects the apocalyptic model as the appropriate way to understand Jesus' eschatological language.

Following in the tradition of Vermes and Smith, the charismatic aspect determines the other models of healer, sage, etc. The ancients believed in two worlds, an everyday world and a spirit-filled world. For them, the spirit world was the "real" one, while for us it tends not to exist, to be suspect, or to be at a distance. "[T]he heart of the biblical tradition is 'charismatic,' its origin lying in the experience of Spirit-endowed people who became radically open to the other world and whose gifts were extraordinary." Jesus was extraordinarily open to this other world, this spirit reality. Borg, for example, takes the baptism and resulting vision along with the testing as historical. "Indeed, the sequence of initiation into the world of the Spirit (the baptism) followed by a testing or ordeal in the wilderness is strikingly similar to what is reported of charismatic figures cross-culturally."[63] Borg here marks a methodological fault line running through the third stage. Does the model (or models) derive from the data or does the model determine what the data is? Sanders clearly belongs to the first group, which is why he looks so assiduously for a sure foundation and finally settles on the canonical line of John the Baptist, Jesus, and Paul. Borg belongs to the latter group.

Borg seems little concerned with issues of authenticity. What fits with the model of the charismatic is judged as somehow historical. His treatment of the baptism illustrates this. The sequence of baptism/ initiation and testing is judged historical because it fits the cross-cultural model of the charismatic. Likewise, "about the historicity of the baptism and the vision itself, there is little reason for doubt," although one could doubt the heavenly voice since it coheres so well with post-Easter Christology. However, if *beloved son* "is given the meaning which similar expressions have in stories of other Jewish charismatic holy men, then it is historically possible to imagine this as part of the experience of Jesus."[64] One of the weaknesses of the criterion of dissimilarity is that it relies on an interpretive model to indicate what is dissimilar. As the example of the heavenly voice indicates, if *beloved son* means "unique son of God," then one would judge the heavenly voice as later. But Borg attempts to construct an argument that makes it historically plausible. Yet the most important question is whether it should be so interpreted in this situation, not just whether it can. This is precisely the question that has plagued the third stage in its effort to overcome the gulf between Jesus and the Gospels.

One of Borg's important contributions is his discussion of the politics of holiness and Jesus' response to it. This developed out of his doctoral dissertation and a later monograph. Borg sees the politics of holiness as a response to the situation of Roman occupation, thus taking a longer view as the context for Jesus the Jew. As a further development of the "holiness code," it sought to answer the question how Israel could be holy while occupied by Rome. Holiness was equated with separation from all that would defile holiness. "The Jewish social world and its conventional wisdom became increasingly structured around the polarities of holiness as separation: clean and unclean, purity and defilement, sacred and profane, Jew and Gentile, righteous and sinner."[65]

A politics of holiness gave rise to a number of renewal movements, among them the Essenes and the Pharisees. Jesus responded to this politics of holiness as separation with a politics of compassion that emphasized inclusiveness. "Just as God is moved by and 'feels with' the 'least of these,' so the Jesus movement was to participate in the pathos of God. Indeed, the pathos of God as compassion was to be the ethos of the Jesus movement and, ideally, of Israel."[66] The politics of compassion is open to all. Borg builds on the picture of Jesus as a teacher of subversive wisdom that had emerged from the study of the parables, referred to above, and the aphorisms, as well as his social practice of inclusion at meals.[67]

While Borg should be applauded for situating Judaism and Jesus within the larger conflict of the Roman Empire, the politics of holiness versus a politics of compassion seems to be a straw man. It stacks the deck against Judaism. Since Borg is unconcerned with issues of authenticity, he does not have to demonstrate that Jesus preached compassion. The model justifies its conclusion. Yet compassion seems to be more a theme of Matthew's Gospel than Jesus' preaching. But Borg has put his finger on an important question—the centrality of the purity code in first-century Judaism.

Borg has advertised what he takes to be a consensus in the third quest that Jesus' message was noneschatological (i.e., that he did not expect the end of the world).[68] I am not sure how a consensus is established,[69] and certainly of those studied to this point, Sanders as well as Vermes would not join such a consensus, although Helmut Koester has recently acknowledged the consensus.[70] Borg's announcement, coupled with the work of Crossan and the Jesus Seminar, has set off a firestorm of debate on this issue.

Borg correctly notes that the linchpin holding the older consensus together was the so-called future Son of man sayings. As long as these were understood as deriving from the historical Jesus, whether he understood himself as the Son of man or some other future agent, it placed a world-ending eschatology at the debate's center. Sanders clearly recognizes this point and has made a spirited defense of the historicity of the Son of man sayings: "Jesus originally said that the Son of Man would come in the immediate future, while his hearers were alive."[71] But beginning with Perrin's work, the Son of man sayings have increasingly been understood as the product of the early church.[72] Douglas Hare's study seems very convincing on this point.[73] This non-end-of-the-world Jesus has been reinforced further by studies on the kingdom of God and parables and aphorisms, beginning with Dodd and Perrin,[74] that increasingly have rejected such an eschatology as the correct interpretive key and turned toward Jewish wisdom as the proper one.

### Mediterranean Jewish Peasant

John Dominic Crossan's *The Historical Jesus: The Life of a Mediterranean Jewish Peasant* may be the most significant study of Jesus in the twentieth century. Crossan has been prolific and creative throughout his whole career. He has followed *The Historical Jesus* with several important studies, most notably *The Birth of Christianity*.

If Sanders's *Jesus and Judaism* represents the historian's quest for the historical Jesus, Crossan's *Historical Jesus* represents the fullest treatment to date of what might be called an interdisciplinary quest. It also demonstrates how controversial this third stage of the quest can be, for it envisions a radically different reconstruction of early Christianity. In that sense, Crossan follows in the footsteps of Strauss. Crossan's methodology is consciously interdisciplinary. It involves

> the reciprocal interplay of a macrocosmic level using cross-cultural and cross-temporal social anthropology, a mesocosmic level using Hellenistic or Greco-Roman history, and a microcosmic level using the literature of specific sayings and deeds, stories and

anecdotes, confessions and interpretations of Jesus. All three levels, anthropological, historical, and literary, must cooperate fully and equally for an effective synthesis.[75]

Crossan came to this study after producing a significant body of work on the sayings tradition,[76] and so he does not share Sanders's distrust of it. Yet he too seeks a firm foundation on which to build his study. Crossan arrives at his foundation by constructing an inventory of the Jesus tradition. Unlike most scholars who restrict their analysis to the Gospels or the synoptics, Crossan casts his net across all the extant literature of Christianity prior to 150 C.E. These documents are then arranged in strata according to their time of composition.[77] Crossan constructs four strata: 30–60, 60–80, 80–120, 120–150 C.E. After the documents are stratified, he then constructs a database of the Jesus tradition built around clusters of similar sayings, ideas, etc. He thereby lays out a stratigraphy of the Jesus tradition. "Plural attestation in the first stratum pushes the trajectory back as far as it can go with at least formal objectivity."[78] This use of multiple attestation within the strata marks a rejection of the criterion of dissimilarity.

In the first stratum, Crossan places not only the letters of Paul, but a number of noncanonical documents (the Gospel of Thomas and the Hebrews) as well as Q, the miracles collection, and the so-called Cross Gospel.[79] Not only are some of these documents noncanonical, but others are hypothetical reconstructions (Q and the Cross Gospel). This favoring of Q and now Thomas continues a line of argument seen in Borg.

While Crossan's investment of the model has generated a great deal of debate,[80] his stratigraphy and reconstructions are not based on eccentric scholarship. For example, he follows closely Kloppenborg on Q[81] and Patterson on the Gospel of Thomas.[82] However, those who prefer the canonical line as Sanders does strongly reject this "favoring" of hypothetical and noncanonical documents. John Meier, in his prolegomena to his study of Jesus, strongly resists the notion of the independence of the Gospel of Thomas from the canonical Gospels. For him, Thomas only makes sense in light of the gnostic myth of the second century.[83] Yet using this same methodology, one could easily show that the Gospel of John is a second-century gnostic text. The question is not whether a document can be understood as gnostic. Works of Plato were found in the Nag Hammadi library. The question is whether that is the appropriate background for interpretation. Furthermore, there are formal issues to be considered. Conspicuously absent in Thomas's version of sayings with a synoptic parallel are the clear redactional elements that would indicate borrowing.[84] The imaginative power of narrative makes it difficult to understand how one could or would construct a sayings gospel by completely eliminating the narrative element. While the use of noncanonical material will remain a significant debating point, I suspect that a theological prejudice in favor of the canon is the real issue.

Crossan's stratigraphy organizes the order in which the data are to be analyzed, but he still must argue his case. For example, Crossan rejects the cluster with the second highest score, "Jesus' Apocalyptic Return." In his reconstruction, it is an early postcrucifixion development that employs Daniel 7:13 as a way of understanding how the scenario of the death and resurrection will play itself out.

Under this methodology, Crossan sometimes evaluates positively what previously had been evaluated negatively. This demonstrates the openness of his method since he takes what is presented to him, not just what would build a case. His treatment of the miracle tradition is a case in point, and shows his consistency with others in the third stage. Free healing is a major building block in his reconstruction.

Crossan at times also uses the evidence of attestation and stratigraphy negatively. For example, in dealing with the apocalyptic Son of man sayings, the fact that they only have single attestation and then not from the early stages is a strong indication that they are inauthentic.[85] A strong criticism of the criterion of dissimilarity, which Crossan also eschews, is that it produces an eccentric Jesus, one at odds with his culture and the tradition that followed. One could also question whether Crossan's dual reliance on early stratigraphy and multiple attestation does not reward the atypical and useful. Or to paraphrase Walter Ong, folks in an oral culture must think memorable thoughts.[86] Nevertheless, while all efforts to deal with the criteria for authenticity have been tricky, the patterning that results from the use of stratigraphy and attestation is potentially very promising. What remains to be worked out is what goes into the various layers of the stratigraphy. For example, if one puts both Paul and Q in the first layer and privileges that layer, then the force of Sanders's canonical line is severely questioned and relativized.

Crossan takes the long view in constructing the background against which to understand the sayings his method presents. He views Jesus and Judaism from the point of view of an anthropological and historical reconstruction of life in the Roman Empire. The three main parts of his book clearly exhibit this model. Part 1 examines the brokered empire that sets up the social environment, the Roman empire, and the anthropological model of brokerage for the distribution of power in the empire.[87] Part 2 deals with tensions created by power in the Roman Empire and various strategies for dealing with that tension. Here the studies of Richard Horsley play a major role.[88] In the final part, Crossan turns to Jesus' option of a brokerless kingdom. Thus, like Borg, his model is deeply political. At the heart of the Jesus movement Crossan sees meals and healing.

> The missionaries do not carry a bag because they do not beg for alms or food or clothing or anything else. They share a miracle and a Kingdom, and they receive in return a table and a house. Here, I think, is the heart of the original Jesus movement, a shared egalitarianism of spiritual and material resources.[89]

The most revolutionary aspect of Crossan's *Historical Jesus* may be that it marks the end of traditional historical criticism as that discipline has been practiced in New Testament studies since the Enlightenment. Crossan's work exemplifies a convergence of a number of currents in recent New Testament scholarship that challenge the status quo of historical criticism—anthropology, sociology, and literary criticism. One should distinguish Crossan's formal methodological proposals from his material investment of the models. The formal model demands serious consideration. Scholars who disagree with his investment should supply their own to determine if it makes a substantial difference. But he also continues the tradition of Reimarus and Schweitzer in that his Jewish peasant would be more at home in the barrios and base communities of South America than in the bourgeois parishes of North American Christianity.

## A Marginal Jew

John Meier has published two-thirds of his monumental study, *A Marginal Jew: Rethinking the Historical Jesus*. A third volume has been announced. Meier is encyclopedic in that every piece of data is carefully sifted, yet his historicism is very traditional and he ignores methods he does not understand or with which he is unsympathetic. Advances in literary criticism and social studies are absent. Meier takes a close view, focusing on the data itself, never really stepping back for a middle or long view.

Meier chose the title "Marginal Jew" as a "tease-word" to suggest various ways of understanding Jesus. Jesus was a "blip on the radar screen" of the ancient world, and he marginalized himself by being "jobless" and by his teachings and practice. "Jesus' style of preaching was thus offensive to many Jews. . . . [A] poor layman from the Galilean countryside with disturbing doctrines and claims was marginal both in the sense of being dangerously antiestablishment and in the sense of lacking a power base in the capital."[90]

To guide his method he images a group of scholars, "a Catholic, a Protestant, a Jew, and an agnostic," locked up in the Harvard Divinity School library who argue out the issues until they reach a consensus. The hermeneutics of historiography are highly debated today,[91] and Meier, like Sanders, comes down on the side of positivism. His goal of objectivity is laudable, but to believe that he can represent these players is a bit naive. Furthermore, his conviction that he can so clearly distinguish between what he knows by history and faith, that he can change a historian's hat for a theologian's, leads to problematic conclusions, at times to an "intellectual agnosticism."[92] Like most third questers, Meier gives the miracle tradition a high prominence. His work on the wonder tradition defines the maximum that a critical historian can claim. He argues, "a historian must reject an apriori affirmation that miracles do not and cannot happen."[93]

Criteria are at the heart of Meier's historical program. He distinguishes five primary criteria. The criterion of embarrassment "focuses on actions or sayings of Jesus that would have embarrassed or created difficulty for the early Church." The criterion of discontinuity focuses on what "cannot be derived either from Judaism at the time of Jesus or from the early Church after him." Without care this criterion leads to "a caricature by divorcing Jesus from the Judaism that influenced him and from the Church that he influenced." The criterion of multiple attestation deals with material attested in more than one independent literary source "and/or more than one literary form or genre." "The criterion of coherence asserts that other sayings and deeds of Jesus that fit in well with the preliminary 'data base' established by using our first three criteria have a good chance of being historical." Finally, Meier develops the criterion of rejection and execution. This criterion pays "attention to the historical fact that Jesus met a violent end at the hands of Jewish and Roman officials and then asks us what historical words and deeds of Jesus can explain his trial and crucifixion as 'King of the Jews.'"[94]

The first four criteria are rather traditional and hardly move beyond Perrin's development or William O. Walker's, to whom Meier frequently refers positively. The final criterion is in line with Sanders and makes Jesus' end the hallmark. Meier stresses that these criteria are strongest when used in conjunction with each other. But the real problem is how they interrelate with his analogy of a group of scholars in the Harvard Divinity School library and his understanding of the separation of faith and history as ways of knowing. Meier's treatment of the virgin birth is a good example. Meier is well aware of the problems of sources in dealing with the infancy stories. But whereas some scholars would dismiss them as adding practically nothing to our knowledge of the historical Jesus, he would not. "According to the two-source theory, Matthew and Luke did not know each other's Gospels; moreover, . . . Matthew's and Luke's Infancy Narratives largely diverge from and even contradict each other. Hence, any agreements between Matthew and Luke in their Infancy Narratives become historically significant."[95] The criterion of multiple attestation sorts out this material as historical. Meier ignores the probability of coincidence, and since for him multiple attestation is an absolute, the mere fact of multiple attestation is significant. But the question remains, what is the significance of multiple attestation when the two witnesses are post-70 C.E.? History or nonhistory are his only explanations. Crossan's stratigraphy in combination with multiple attestation is more discriminating and powerful.

Applied to the virgin birth, again multiple attestation indicates that it is not a "late legend." Pagan myths are ruled out as not parallel enough, and so "historical-critical research simply does not have the sources and tools available to reach a final decision on the historicity of the virginal conception." The wall between history and faith means that "one's acceptance or rejection of the doctrine will be largely influenced by one's own philosophical and theological presuppositions, as well as the weight one gives Church teaching."[96] I wonder whether anyone besides the Catholic locked in the library of the Harvard Divinity School got a vote on that one. The fundamental problem with Meier's use of his criteria is that they really do not sort the data, but reinforce a rather traditional portrait of Jesus.

Meier surveys the sources available to the historian with great thoroughness. But whereas he is quite open to the possibility of the Gospel of John containing historical material (e.g., the longer, three-year ministry), he rejects the Gospel of Thomas. If the Gospel of Thomas is gnostic, Meier's reason for rejecting it, then so is the Gospel of John and so both should be either considered or rejected. The poor agnostic must have lost a lot of votes in Meier's Harvard group.

So strongly does Meier support what I have termed Sanders's canonical line (John the Baptist, Jesus, and Paul) that some 230 pages of his second volume are devoted to John the Baptist and Jesus. The "Mentor" in the second volume's subtitle is John the Baptist, "the one person who had the greatest single influence on Jesus' ministry." John was an apocalyptic prophet of an imminent end and he expected "a stronger one" to come after him. John baptized Jesus and for a time Jesus was his disciple. While shifts and differences did appear between Jesus and John, "Yet a firm substratum of the Baptist's message and life remained; and as far as we know, it remained throughout Jesus' ministry."[97]

John the Baptist as mentor leads directly to Jesus' message. Since Jesus follows John, Jesus' message, too, is primarily apocalyptic. For Meier, Jesus preaches the kingdom of God. "His choice of it as a key theme is just that:

a conscious, personal choice, and for that reason the symbol is a privileged way of entering into Jesus' message." This being the case, Meier's first task is to determine what his symbol means. He notes that the phrase "kingdom of God" is multiply attested in the Jesus tradition, but "the precise phrase 'kingdom of God' does not occur as such in the Hebrew Old Testament, and occurrences in the deuterocanonical/ apocryphal books of the Old Testament, the Old Testament pseudepigrapha, Qumran, Philo, Josephus, and most of the targums are either rare or nonexistent."[98]

Meier deals with this lack of evidence by redefining the symbol as the concept of God ruling as king, for which there is abundant evidence. Thus, Meier's confidence is high that "the kingdom of God does not have a definition; it tells a story." He provides a "fast-forwarding" through a summary of this "mythic story" that "stretches from the first page of the Bible to its last." Significantly, "depending upon how apocalyptic a given storyteller might be, the final kingdom might be envisioned as a restoration-but-vast improvement of David's original kingdom, or a return to paradise on earth, or a heavenly kingdom beyond this world of time and space."[99] Thus, the kingdom of God is a mythic and apocalyptic summary of Israel's experience of God as king.

With the symbol of the kingdom of God so predetermined as apocalyptic, Meier's first example and archetype for Jesus' message is the Lord's prayer, especially "your kingdom come." Both multiple attestation and discontinuity indicate that the prayer is authentic. Its highly liturgical character does not cause Meier pause or concern.

Meier also sees that in certain sayings the kingdom is present. Luke 11:20 is his best example. This is a particularly important saying for Meier because it combines the presence of the kingdom with Jesus' exorcisms: "But if by the finger of God I cast out demons then upon you has come the kingdom of God." His conclusion concerning this saying is significant: "Jesus does present his exorcisms as proof that the kingdom of God that he proclaims for the future is in some sense already present." What does "in some sense" mean? To Meier's credit he does not try to ignore this saying, as does Sanders. "How this [the presence of the kingdom] coheres—or whether it coheres—with what Jesus says about the kingdom soon to come remains an open question."[100]

In a number of places Meier struggles with how to reconcile this tension. In noting the difference between John the Baptist who preached a future kingdom and Jesus, Meier states:

> On the one hand, Jesus makes the kingdom of God, not himself, the direct object of his preaching. Yet what he says about the kingdom and what he promises those who enter it by accepting his message make a monumental though implicit claim: with the start of Jesus' ministry, a definitive shift has taken place in the eschatological timetable.

In attempting to summarize this argument he concludes: "The important point, in my view, is that Jesus consciously chose to indicate that the display of miraculous power in his own ministry constituted a partial and preliminary realization of God's kingly rule, which would soon be displayed in full force."[101]

In his struggle between a kingdom in the future and in the present, Meier stands alone among third stage scholars. While he leans toward Sanders in seeing the future as dominant, he does not dismiss the present kingdom.

The starting point for a question is often critical in determining the answer. Meir privileges the kingdom of God as the entrance point but then determines the meaning of the phrase from his reconstruction of the mythic story of God as king. His reconstruction compels an apocalyptic reading of the myth. Yet if he privileges kingdom of God, why does he not also privilege the parables, which were Jesus' vehicle for the kingdom? His reasoning seems to be that parables are an inappropriate vehicle for the kingdom: "[R]ecent scholarship, by approaching the parables as autonomous pieces of rhetorical art, has reminded us how open is each parable to multiple interpretations—at least if taken by itself, in isolation from the rest of Jesus' message and praxis."[102] Unless this is meant as an ad hominem argument against contemporary parable scholarship, then the force of Meier's argument would be that Jesus made a mistake in employing parables as a vehicle for the kingdom. But perhaps parable tells us something important about the symbol of the kingdom of God.

While Meier stands alone in trying to reconcile these two elements in the kingdom, he is probably correct in rejecting the either/or distinction. The categories we are currently working with are inadequate to the discussion. We must look forward to the promised third volume, where perhaps Meier can reconcile this tension when he turns to Jesus' own self-understanding.

### The Return from Exile

If it is difficult to present a final evaluation of Meier because there is yet one more, I presume large, volume to come, the problem is even more difficult with N. T. Wright. His *Jesus and the Victory of God* is the second volume of a proposed five-volume series dealing with Christian origins and the question of God. Since Wright's reconstruction is the most divergent surveyed, summarization becomes difficult. Wright's program will appeal to traditionalists who want to maintain the historicity of the Gospels, until they reflect on what they will have to surrender.

Wright stands in opposition to Enlightenment currents, which he views as pessimistic and skeptical, and employs a methodology he terms "critical realism." The other scholars in this review all fall within the trajectory stemming from the Enlightenment. To one degree or another, they accept the methods of historiography that have developed and evolved out of the Enlightenment. They employ a hermeneutics of suspicion. For my part, the gains of the Enlightenment in terms of scientific method are permanent, understanding that built into scientific method is a continuous correcting process of which the history of the quest is an example. I have tried to indicate at various places in this essay what I consider to be permanent gains for the quest of the historical Jesus. For example, those gains demonstrating the fictional character of the Gospel outlines (e.g., Wrede and K. L. Schmidt) and the fragmentary and oral nature of the tradition prior to the Gospels place limitations on the nature of research. Wright ultimately rejects not only the methods of the Enlightenment, but also the gains of the quest to this point. Therefore, in the end, I simply cannot take his project seriously. It is symptomatic of the loss of nerve that seems to infect parts of the West at this crucial time in history. Because I reject his project, however, does not meant that I cannot learn from it.

I will briefly describe Wright's method and then offer an example that I hope will fairly illuminate both his method and position.

Critical realism "acknowledges the essentially 'storied' nature of human knowing, thinking, and living, within the larger model of worldviews and their component parts. It acknowledges that all knowledge of realities external to oneself takes place within the framework of a worldview, of which stories form an essential part."[103] In what potentially may yield an important insight, Wright proposes to construct the worldview of first-century Judaism. Wright distinguishes four characteristics of a worldview: "characteristic stories; fundamental symbols; habitual praxis; and a set of questions and answers" about the basic issues of life, such as, "who are we? . . . what's wrong?"[104] In *The New Testament and the People of God*, Wright constructs the worldview of first-century Judaism.

From here, Wright proceeds to discuss the subject of mindsets. A mindset is "a worldview held by a particular individual person."[105] Interesting people frequently have mindsets in which elements are at variance with the worldview in which they reside. In *Jesus and the Victory of God*, Wright reconstructs the mindset of Jesus.

The worldview of Judaism and the mindset of Jesus function as a hypothesis to explain Christian origins, or the stories early Christians told about themselves. "It [critical realism] sets up as hypotheses various stories about the world in general or bits of it in particular and tests them by seeing what sort of 'fit' they have with the stories already in place."[106] Such a hypothesis is prior to the sorting of the data and is meant to explain the data. The more data it can explain, the better the hypothesis. Thus, Wright's critical realism turns the assumption of Enlightenment scientific method on its head. The hypothesis explains the data, rather than emerging from the data.

At the risk of oversimplification, a major element according to Wright in the worldview of first-century Judaism is the experience of exile. First-century Jews viewed themselves as exiled from and abandoned by God: "They believed that, in all the senses which mattered, Israel's exile was still in progress." This is the "what is wrong?" of the worldview. The Roman occupation of Israel reinforced the notion of abandonment. Even though the temple had been rebuilt, God had not returned to dwell in it. "[U]ntil the Gentiles are put in their place and Israel, and the Temple, fully restored, the exile is not really over, and the blessings promised by the prophets are still to take place."[107]

Wright sees Jesus as "a prophet like the prophets of old, coming to Israel with a word from her covenant god, warning her of the imminent and fearful consequences of the direction she was traveling, urging and summoning her to a new and different way." While Jesus expects an apocalyptic end, he, like his "contemporaries who were looking for a great event to happen in the immediate future were not expecting the end of the space-time universe," but the end of a particular world.[108]

Jesus' mindset resolves the fundamental issues of the Jewish world-view. "Jesus was announcing that the long-awaited kingdom of Israel's god was indeed coming to birth. . . . The return from exile, the defeat of evil, and the return of YHWH to Zion were all coming about, but not in the way Israel had supposed." This mindset explains the Jesus tradition. The miracles of Jesus are prophetic signs "inaugurating the long-awaited time of liberations, the return from exile, the kingdom of Israel's god." The Son of man sayings depict not a being coming to earth from heaven, but, Wright argues, the other way around, as in Daniel, 7: "He comes from earth to heaven, vindicated after suffering."[109]

Wright's analysis of Mark 13 is a good example of his method and his employment of Jesus' mindset as a hypothesis. Despite the scholarly consensus that Mark 13 was written after the destruction of Jerusalem, Wright sees it as essentially coming from Jesus: "[W]e will discover that it possesses an inner coherence and that it draws together exactly that combination of warnings and promises which we have seen to characterize Jesus' ministry all through."[110]

The disciples had gone "to Jerusalem expecting Jesus to be enthroned as the rightful king." Now they heard the news that "the Temple's destruction would constitute his own vindication." Thus, Jesus was speaking about his own vindication "both as a prophet and as the one who has the right to pronounce upon the Temple, and . . . as the actual replacement for the Temple." The followers of Jesus were to flee at the time of the destruction because they had been forewarned. "Their vindication will come when the city that has opposed Jesus is destroyed."[111]

While Wright sees Jesus weaving together a host of Old Testament texts in the construction of Mark 13, two in particular stand out— Daniel and 1 Maccabees. The Maccabees had used the Daniel story "in order to make it clear that the events of 167 B.C. were to be seen as the fulfillment of prophecy." Likewise, Jesus is recycling the Danielic and Maccabean prophecies to apply to the Roman situation. These recycled prophecies "would naturally be read in the first century in terms not of Syrian invasion but of Roman." But Jesus redefines the scenario with a difference. He identifies, according to Wright, "the forces opposing the true people of god [i.e., the disciples], not with Rome, but with present Jerusalem and its hierarchy." Jesus speaks "as only some extreme sectarians would speak, of Jerusalem and the Temple as the real enemy, and of a little group, around a prophetic figure, as the true people of Israel. It is profoundly similar to the outlook we find in the early church."[112]

For Wright, the prophecies of Mark 13 are "the necessary and predictable focal point of Jesus' whole prophetic ministry." As such they summarize Jesus' ministry. "As the kingdom-bearer, he had constantly been acting . . . in a way which invited the conclusion that he thought he had the right to do and be what the Temple was and did, thereby making the Temple redundant." The kingdom of God was the liberation from exile, and Jesus was a prophet, king, messiah, and temple. The true people of Israel were Jesus' followers, and the enemy was the hierarchy in Jerusalem, those unfaithful Jews who had rejected Jesus, and Rome's destruction of the temple would vindicate Jesus and prove him a true prophet.[113] "As prophet, Jesus staked his reputation on his prediction of the temple's fall within a generation; if and when it fell, he would be vindicated."[114] For Wright, Jesus predicted the destruction of the Temple and he was thus vindicated. Schweitzer's charge that Jesus was an apocalyptic prophetic expecting the end of the space-time continuum is untrue. Likewise, the effort of some to understand Mark 13 as the Church's expectation of Jesus' second coming is wrong. Jesus and the early church were right and this proves it.

This is a strong hypothesis for Wright because "it includes the data."[115] The totalizing power of the hypothesis to explain so much, almost all, of the data is most seductive. Gone are the sometimes tedious shifting and reconstruction in the work of Crossan and Meier. Yet the seduction should be resisted. The very profound similarity "to the outlook we find in the early church"[116] should lead one to pause. Does apocalyptic ever produce genuine prophecy? Wright notes that Mark 13 is made up of a pastiche or interweaving of biblical texts and that his two principal texts, Daniel and Maccabees, both employ the story of past events to look back at a recent past. For example, Daniel uses the Babylonians to understand the Syrians. If the authors of Daniel and Maccabees use past events to understand the present, would it not make more sense to see Christian apocalyptic preachers using the same set of stories to make sense of Rome's destruction of the temple? Why assume that Jesus is using these texts in a genuine prophecy (fore-telling), when the history and genre of apocalyptic is to look back?

Furthermore and most importantly, the figure of the Son of man in Daniel is clearly ascending rather than descending. In 1 Thess 4:16–17, Paul uses the Son of man as descending. Finally, there is little or no evidence that first-century Judaism understood itself as in exile. These are not trivial points but major cornerstones in Wright's reconstruction of the worldview of Judaism and the mindset of Jesus.

### Jesus by Committee

Any review of the third stage must deal with the Jesus Seminar. Its founder, Robert Funk, however, does not see the work of the Seminar as part of the third stage, but as the "ReNewed Quest" for Jesus.[117] Yet the Jesus Seminar is largely responsible for the public attention that historical Jesus scholarship has drawn in the media and for stimulating much of the debate concerning the historical Jesus. Some of that debate has been quite acrimonious. I cannot claim to be an impartial observer of the Seminar since I am a charter member and was coeditor of the Seminar's first publication.[118] So let the reader beware.

The Seminar also cannot really be considered in the same way as the other scholars reviewed, two of whom (Borg and Crossan) are members. The Seminar does not speak with one voice, but records votes. There is not one mind guiding the Seminar, as is the case in every other study here surveyed. The votes represent shifting alliances, minds changing, doubt. Sometimes the outcome of a vote has depended upon who showed up. Therefore, there is at times a certain inconsistency in the Seminar's votes. The votes represent a range of positions within a group of scholars. It is not a matter of winner takes all or that the one with the most votes is right. A picture of the historical Jesus does emerge from the votes of the Seminar, but the Seminar has yet, and probably cannot, set out a single, unified portrait of Jesus.

The Jesus Seminar began in 1985 when Robert Funk sent out an invitation to scholars to join him in a renewal of the quest of the historical Jesus and to report the outcome to the general public. From the very beginning, the Seminar had an educational goal—to make the results of scholarship available to anyone who was interested. Initially, thirty scholars showed up in Berkeley, California, for the first meeting. Ultimately, about two hundred scholars were involved in the project, seventy-four of whom signed off on *The Five Gospels: The Search for the Authentic Words of Jesus*. The Seminar also began a scholarly journal, *Forum*, to report its debates and conversations.

According to *The Five Gospels*, the report of the Jesus Seminar, their first step "was to inventory and classify all the words attributed to Jesus in the first three centuries of the common era."[119] This inventory was published as *Sayings Parallels: A Workbook for the Jesus Tradition* (Crossan, 1986).[120] The procedure for the Seminar's sessions followed a consistent pattern. Sayings were assigned, papers were written and published, then discussed and debated, and finally the scholars voted.

The original proposal had been that the voting would be a simple yes or no. Using the analogy of red-letter Bibles, those sayings that were voted yes would be printed in red. But this proposal soon proved unworkable. More options were needed to express the levels of certainty and uncertainty, and so each option was further subdivided. Red was divided into red and pink, and black into black and gray. There never was complete agreement on what the four colors signified.[121]

In contrast to the rest of the third stage, the Jesus Seminar began with the sayings. There were several reasons for this, some of which were theoretical and others pragmatic. Funk viewed the Seminar as a renewal of the New Quest. More importantly, Rudolf Bultmann, in the most important study of the synoptic tradition of the twentieth century, *The History of the Synoptic Tradition*, had divided the Gospel material into two parts: the sayings of Jesus and narrative material. This division set the agenda for the Seminar.[122] The first stage ended in the publication of *The Five Gospels*, and the second in *The Acts of Jesus*. At the beginning, we had no realistic idea how long it would take to survey and vote on the material. Almost everyone estimated a much shorter time than it actually took. At the time, I was finishing a commentary on the parables,[123] and so was in a position to produce an essay surveying issues of authenticity about the parables.[124]

The Seminar is a good example of the importance of a starting point. The parables produced a large number of red and pink votes, with the Leaven, the Good Samaritan, Dishonest Steward, and the Vineyard Laborers all receiving red votes. To scholars who have followed parable studies, there was nothing particularly surprising in the outcome. The Seminar was not concerned about the meaning or interpretation of a parable, only with its authenticity.

By beginning with the parables, two important issues came to the fore. The parables accented the wisdom tradition, and the Gospel of Thomas received independent consideration. In parable studies, this was not a controversial position, since Jeremias in the sixth German edition (1962) of his influential book on the parables had acknowledged that the parables in Thomas were independent witnesses.[125] Over a period of time and debate, the dominant position in the Seminar became that not only were the parables in Thomas independent, but so was the entire Gospel of Thomas. Also, beginning with the parables led the Seminar to stress multiple attestation rather than dissimilarity. This may seem strange since so many of the parables appear just once, but the form itself is multiply attested.

Soon the apocalyptic issue was joined. It became evident that a majority of the Seminar members did not think that Jesus was an apocalyptic thinker. The reasons for this were multiple, but the two dominant ones were the parables (the point where we had started) and the recent studies on Q. John Kloppenborg, a member of the Seminar, had just produced an important study of Q arguing that it was composed of layers of which the earliest was wisdom. Apocalyptic was the latest addition to Q.[126] The votes began to indicate a definite preference in the Seminar for a wisdom rather than an apocalyptic Jesus. Unfortunately, many of those who supported the apocalyptic position gradually quit attending the Seminar sessions.

The Jesus Seminar has proven to be quite controversial, probably because it went public. The Seminar should probably be viewed as an educational enterprise. Its purpose from the beginning was to make the results of scholarship readily available to the general public, something scholars seldom do. Frequently, the headlines were shocking to those who were unfamiliar with biblical scholarship, which, unfortunately, is most of the population.

The controversy in response to the Seminar has been loud and vociferous. There has been a predictable critique from the right,[127] those who espouse a Kähler-like position,[128] and from those who differ with the Seminar's nonapocalyptic Jesus.[129] There has also been a response within the Jesus Seminar.[130] Fleshing out this debate is well beyond the scope of this survey, but I recommend that interested readers consult Mark Powell, who has in my judgment produced the fairest and most balanced analysis of the work of the Jesus Seminar and the debate that surrounds it. He concludes:

> What marks the Jesus Seminar as unique—probably the *only* thing that marks them as unique—is that they are a group. Though other scholars may confer with colleagues, only the Jesus Seminar has invested the time, money, and energy to meet so regularly and under such circumstances that their publications can truly be termed the work of the whole group. This is not an inconsiderable accomplishment, and this fact alone earns them the attention they have received.[131]

### Millenarian Prophet

The studies of Crossan, Borg, and the Jesus Seminar have provoked a spirited defense of the apocalyptic position. None of these studies move significantly beyond the position of Sanders, although each gives a new accent to the position. For that reason my treatment of them will be very brief.

In *Jesus of Nazareth: Millenarian Prophet*, Dale Allison argues that the material must be approached with hypothesis already in place, and for him the hypothesis is that Jesus was a millenarian prophet. He develops a very interesting phenomenological typology from cross-cultural analysis of the millenarianism and shows how it applies to Jesus. Allison rejects Wright's contention that Jesus' expectation of the end of the world was metaphorical. Allison contends that Jesus expected the end of the time-space continuum. Bart Ehrman, in *Jesus: Apocalyptic Prophet of the New Milennium*, takes a similar position. Paula Fredriksen, in *Jesus of Nazareth, King of the Jews*, returns to Sanders's original insight on the death of Jesus. That is the single fact that most needs explanation. She also advances the question of the purity code within Judaism, an issue that is very important and needs further development.[132]

## Conclusions

There are a number of characteristics of this third stage of the quest that hold true of all the investigators, despite their differences.

(1) All are seeking a historical explanation of Jesus, and the critical issue is to explain the totality of Jesus' activity, not just his message. This includes the death of Jesus and the subsequent rise of early Christianity. Accents vary with each author, but the effort to furnish a comprehensive model is characteristic. Vermes and Smith are more narrow in this regard with mainly univocal models, and Borg and Crossan have the richest mix. Sanders in his first volume explicitly sets out to solve the riddle of the cause of Jesus' death; for Meier it is criterion of authenticity, and Fredriksen has returned yet again to the centrality of the crucifixion in any explanation of Jesus. Ultimately, they all argue that it was his subversive, provocative actions, not his words, that led to the confrontation with the authorities.

(2) The accent falls on the miracle tradition, not the sayings. Again there are variations with Sanders and Crossan representing the richest mix and the strongest contrast. Sanders almost repudiates the sayings tradition, and, for him, the deeds interpret the sayings. Crossan's stratification method forces him to deal with the sayings in a primary way, although his model is not that of teacher. Meier's painstaking analysis of the wonder tradition delineates the most that a historian can claim.

Despite this shift in emphasis, the deeds fail to furnish a firm foundation. Isolating the deeds from their redactional context and providing them with a sure interpretive foundation is no easier, and perhaps harder, than dealing with the sayings tradition. Furthermore, rejecting the rich exegetical tradition built up around the parables, proverbs, and kingdom sayings impoverishes the studies. This distrust of words as evidenced by Sanders and Meier is hard to justify. Perhaps the following acid remark by Maier reflects his own impotency in a capitalist society rather than an objective assessment of words in the ancient world: "A tweedy poetaster who spent his time spinning out parables and Japanese koans, a literary aesthete who toyed with 1st century deconstructionism, or a bland Jesus who simply told people to look at the lilies of the field—such a Jesus would threaten no one, just as the university professors who create him threaten no one."[133] Socrates, next to Jesus one of the most famous martyrs of the ancient world, died because of his provocative language, and the problems of Salman Rushdie in our own day demonstrate the power of words in a traditional society.

(3) Unlike the previous two stages, which drew sharp distinctions between Jesus, Judaism, and early Christianity, the third stage accents and builds on continuity. The early work of Ben Meyer anticipated this development,[134] and Wright is highly indebted to him. Too often, third stagers in a rush to find continuity and to be less skeptical than previous questers have been too trusting and too naive. On the other hand, the effort to make sense of Jesus within Judaism has been much more successful. Vermes' pioneering work situating Jesus within populist Judaism rather than the elitist Judaism of rabbinicism has proven a very successful interpretive strategy. The social location of Jesus is a major issue. Brad Young's *Jesus and His Jewish Parables* fails precisely at this point when Young turns Jesus into a scribal rabbi instead of a Galilean peasant.[135] To a lesser degree, this problem has beset the important work of Bruce Chilton.[136]

(4) The third stage has shown a rich historical mix of methods and data. While this has been controversial, for example, Smith's use of the magic tradition or Crossan's use of the noncanonical tradition, it is gradually producing a much richer picture of Jesus, Judaisms, and early

Christianities. The contrast between Sanders and Crossan can represent the options. For Sanders, the line between John the Baptist, Jesus, and Paul is straight. For Crossan, there is a break between John and Jesus, and the Q and Thomas follow much more closely on Jesus. Thus, we have a canonical versus a pluralist line. Meier and the apocalypticists support Sanders. This marks a major debate point in the third stage, and its implications for understanding Jesus and the early Christianities cannot be overestimated. A previous generation of scholars attacked and broke down the notion of normative Judaism, arguing that there were a variety of Judaisms.[137] Yet some have reinstituted a new normative Judaism around apocalyptic expectation. This, too, should be resisted. Second temple Judaism and early Christianity were so pluralistic that we will have to decide whether one can speak of Judaism or Judaisms, and of the early Church or only of early communities.

(5) The issue of Christian faith has been a question and problem in the quest since its inauguration with Reimarus. Borg and Sanders take up very different positions on this point. Borg essentially views the quest as part of his own spiritual quest, and this is quite evident in his *Meeting Jesus Again for the First Time.*[138] It begins with one of the most honest exposures by a scholar of his own spiritual quest of which I am aware. Sanders, on the other hand, confesses to his lifelong effort "to free history and exegesis from the control of theology; that is, from being obligated to come to certain conclusions which are pre-determined by theological commitment." How does Sanders's Jesus stand up to his religious tradition? "I am a liberal, modern, secularized Protestant, brought up in a church dominated by low christology and the social gospel. I am proud of the things that religious tradition stands for. I am not bold enough, however, to suppose that Jesus came to establish it, or that he died for the sake of its principles."[139]

Crossan and Meier, both Roman Catholics, represent yet another variation. Meier, somewhat in the tradition of Kähler, draws a sharp distinction between history and faith. He even at times speaks of wearing his historian's hat and then his theologian's hat.[140] After Hans-Georg Gadamer one is tempted to ignore this simplistic and naive distinction, but Meier apparently is serious. History and faith are separate and do not commingle for Meier. Crossan, on the other hand takes a much more analogical approach.[141] He argues, "What happened historically is that those who believed in Jesus before his execution continued to do so afterward."[142] Thus, Crossan posits no sharp wedge, and both history and faith are free to interact. His *Jesus: A Revolutionary Biography* could be understood as historical understanding seeking faith, to play on Anselm's aphorism. Wright represents yet another position in which there is no distinction between history and faith.

(6) A schism within the third stage breaks around what I have termed the canonical versus the pluralist lines. Those in the canonical camp tend to disparage the sayings at the expense of the deeds, paint Jesus' eschatology as apocalyptic, see him as apolitical, and finally take a middle view that focuses on Jesus within Judaism. This clearly describes Sanders, Wright, and Meier. In Meier's view, "Jesus seems to have had no interest in the great political and social questions of his day. He was not interested in the reform of the world because he was prophesying its end."[143] On the other hand, Borg and Crossan, beginning with a long view, portray Jesus in the sapiential mode, thus balancing the deeds and sayings, and present a political Jesus who was concerned with issues of the day. They see both Jesus and Judaism within the context of the Roman Empire.

Another aspect of this schism is the status of Q and the Gospel of Thomas. Scholars who specialize in the Gospel of Thomas have reached a consensus that Thomas is not gnostic, is not dependent on the synoptics, and that the core of the tradition goes back to the first century. Q studies are more problematic. The international Q project appears to be forging a consensus, but there are significant objections.[144] Clearly Q cannot be set aside and does represent a wisdom position in early Christianity. So we have to deal with a pluralistic primitive Christianity. When should we refer to the Jesus movement as a movement, and when should we call it Christian? Until these basic questions can be solved, stratigraphy will be problematic. Despite the deep schism that divides the third stage, the mix is rich enough to develop into a real debate.[145]

(7) Each stage of the quest has sought a firm foundation on which to build. The first sought a solution to the synoptic problem in hopes

that it would produce a basis for a biography of Jesus. The New Quest investigated criteria for authenticity in an effort to certify the sayings tradition. The problem of foundation has plagued the third stage. Sanders selected the temple act as the firm foundation, and Crossan constructed a formal method that intersected stratigraphy with multiple attestation. Meier has carefully sorted all the data, and Wright has created an all-encompassing hypothesis. Others have sought the appropriate background, charismatic Hasid or magician, millenarian prophet or wisdom teacher. The foundation has proven elusive because one cannot dispense with the need for interpretation, and interpretation inevitably introduces doubt, argument, and subjectivity. The historical sciences can never achieve the certainty of the experimental sciences. And so the sure foundation will remain a problem, even if gains are made.

Where to begin is the problem. Does one start with the data (Sanders, Crossan, Meier) or a hypothesis (Borg, Wright, Allison)? I find the latter very problematic because there is no way to certify the hypothesis. This leads to totalizing theories. The question is not whether something can be interpreted by a given hypothesis, but should it? On the other hand, those who begin with the data always face the issue of which data to use. I find more persuasive Crossan's formal method than I do Meier's criteria or Sanders's certain facts. A continued refinement of Crossan's formal method and its investment strikes me as the direction to proceed.

While I obviously favor beginning with the data rather than a hypothesis, this is not a simple either/or process. Rather, it is a dialectic between data and hypothesis, with the hypothesis constantly being checked against the data. Simple hypotheses and univocal models should be avoided. Many of our models come from upper-class, literate culture, and thus are inappropriate for Jesus.

Meier's privileging of the symbol of the kingdom of God is an important step forward. But, how do we know what kingdom of God means? Meier turns to the concept of God as king. But I would suggest that we follow Jesus' own guide and turn to the parables.[146] To use Wright's phrase, the parables are Jesus' mindset. The parables as Jesus' mindset provide the framework to understand the deeds and sayings isolated by formal method.

There have always been efforts to silence the quest of the historical Jesus. Yet it will not go away. For as Schweitzer remarked, the quest "laid down the conditions and determined the course of religious thinking of the future."[147] The prophecy may yet come true.

NOTES

1. Marcus J. Borg, "A Renaissance in Jesus Studies," *Theology Today* 45 (October 1988), 280–92; Stephen Neill and Tom Wright, *The Interpretation of the New Testament 1861–1986*, 2d ed. (Oxford: Oxford University Press, 1988), 379–403; James H. Charlesworth, *Jesus within Judaism* (New York: Doubleday, 1988), 15; E. P. Sanders, Jesus and Judaism (Philadelphia: Fortress Press, 1985), 2.

2. Albert Schweitzer, *The Quest of the Historical Jesus: A Critical Study of Its Progress from Reimarus to Wrede*, trans. W. Montgomery (1906; repr., New York: Macmillan, 1968), 2.

3. See Charles H. Talbert, ed., *Reimarus: Fragments* (Philadelphia: Fortress Press, 1970).

4. Gothold Lessing, *Lessing's Theological Writings*, ed. Henry Chadwick (Stanford, Calif.: Stanford University Press, 1957) 53.

5. Elizabeth L. Eisenstein, *The Printing Press as an Agent of Change: Communications and Cultural Transformations in Early Modern Europe*, vol. 1 (New York: Cambridge University Press, 1979), chap. 4.

6. David Friedrich Strauss, *The Life of Jesus Critically Examined*, ed. Leander Keck (1838; repr., Philadelphia: Fortress Press, 1972).

7. Albert Schweitzer, "The Sanity of the 'Eschatological Jesus,'" *The Expositor*, 8th series, no. 6 (1913): 328–42, 439–55, 554–68; See also Daryl D. Schmidt, "Sane Eschatology: Albert Schweitzer's Profile of Jesus," *Forum*, new series 1 (1998): 241–60.

8. Reprinted in Hans Conzelmann, *Jesus*, trans. J. Raymond Lord (Philadelphia: Fortress Press, 1973) 5.

9. Wilhelm Wrede, *The Messianic Secret* (1901; repr., Greenwood, S.C.: Attic, 1971).

10. K. L. Schmidt, *Der Rahmen der Geschichte Jesu, Literarkritische Untersuchungen zur altesten Jesus-Uberlieferung* (1919; repr. Darmstadt: Wissenschaftliche Buchgesellschaft, 1969).

11. See Rudolf Bultmann, *The History of the Synoptic Tradition* (New York: Harper & Row, 1963); Martin Dibelius, *From Tradition to Gospel*, trans. Bertram Lee Woolf (1919; repr., New York: Charles Scribner's Sons, 1935).

12. Martin Kähler, *The So-Called Historical Jesus and the Historic, Biblical Christ* (1896; repr., Philadelphia: Fortress Press, 1988).

13. Rudolf Bultmann, *Theology of the New Testament*, trans. Kendrick Grobel (New York: Charles Scribner's Sons, 1951, 1955), 1:3.

44 · *Bernard Brandon Scott*

14. James M. Robinson, *A New Quest of the Historical Jesus* (London: SCM Press, 1959).

15. See Paul J. Achtemeier, *An Introduction to the New Hermeneutic* (Philadelphia: Westminster Press, 1969); Robert W. Funk, *Language, Hermeneutic and Word of God* (New York: Harper & Row, 1966).

16. Reprinted in Ernst Käsemann, "The Problem of the Historical Jesus," in *Essays on New Testament Themes* (London: SCM Press, 1964), 213–14.

17. Leander E. Keck, *A Future for the Historical Jesus: The Place of Jesus in Preaching and Theology* (Nashville: Abingdon, 1971), 41–42, note 12.

18. Edward Schillebeeckx, *Jesus: An Experiment in Christology*, trans. Hubert Hoskins (New York: Crossroad, 1981).

19. Norman Perrin, *Rediscovering the Teaching of Jesus* (New York: Harper & Row, 1967), 39.

20. See William O. Walker, "The Quest for the Historical Jesus: A Discussion of Methodology," *Harvard Theological Review* 51 (January 1969): 38–56; Eugene M. Boring, "The Historical-Critical Method's 'Criteria for Authenticity': The Beatitudes in Q and Thomas as a Test Case," *Semeia* 44 (1988): 9–44.

21. Perrin, *Rediscovering the Teaching of Jesus*, 39.

22. Joachim Jeremias, *The Parables of Jesus* (New York: Charles Scribner's Sons, 1972), 9, 12.

23. See Adolf Jülicher, *Die Gleichnisreden Jesu* (1910; repr., Darmstadt: Wissenschaftliche Buchgesellschaft, 1969); C. H. Dodd, *The Parables of the Kingdom* (1935; repr., New York: Charles Scribner's Sons, 1961); Funk, *Language, Hermeneutic and Word of God*; Robert W. Funk, *Jesus as Precursor* (Philadelphia: Fortress Press, 1975); Robert W. Funk, *Parables and Presence* (Philadelphia: Fortress Press, 1982); Dan O. Via Jr., *The Parables: Their Literary and Existential Dimension* (Philadelphia: Fortress Press, 1967); John Dominic Crossan, *In Parables: The Challenge of the Historical Jesus* (New York: Harper & Row, 1973); Bernard Brandon Scott, *Hear Then the Parable: A Commentary on the Parables of Jesus* (Minneapolis: Fortress Press, 1989).

24. Norman Perrin, *The Kingdom of God in the Teaching of Jesus* (London: SCM Press, 1963); Perrin, *Rediscovering the Teaching of Jesus*; Norman Perrin, *Jesus and the Language of the Kingdom: Symbol and Metaphor in New Testament Interpretation* (Philadelphia: Fortress Press, 1976).

25. See Philip Wheelwright, *Metaphor and Reality* (Bloomington, Ind.: Indiana University Press, 1968).

26. See Dennis Duling, "Norman Perrin and the Kingdom of God: Review and Response," *Journal of Religion* 64 (October 1984): 468–83; Erich Grässer, "Norman Perrin's Contribution to the Quest of the Historical Jesus," *Journal of Religion* 64 (October 1984): 484–500.

27. See Johannes Weiss, *Jesus' Proclamation of the Kingdom*, trans. Richard Hiers and David Holland (Philadelphia: Fortress Press, 1971).

28. Geza Vermes, *Jesus the Jew: A Historian's Reading of the Gospels* (London: Collins, 1973). See also Geza Vermes, *Jesus and the World of Judaism* (London:

SCM Press, 1983); Geza Vermes, *The Religion of Jesus the Jew* (Minneapolis: Fortress Press, 1993).

29. Käsemann, "Problem of the Historical Jesus," 38.

30. Vermes, *Jesus the Jew*, 22.

31. But see Paul J. Achtemeier, "Miracles and the Historical Jesus: Mark 9:14–29," *Catholic Biblical Quarterly* 37 (October 1975): 471–91.

32. Vermes, *Jesus the Jew*, 65.

33. Ibid., 73. For a discussion of this same text, see John Dominic Crossan, *The Historical Jesus: The Life of a Mediterranean Jewish Peasant* (San Francisco: HarperSanFrancisco, 1991), 153–56.

34. Vermes, *Religion of Jesus the Jew*, 5.

35. Morton Smith, *Jesus the Magician* (San Francisco: Harper & Row, 1978), 105, 122–23, 150.

36. Morton Smith, *Clement of Alexandria and a Secret Gospel of Mark* (Cambridge, Mass.: Harvard University Press, 1973); Morton Smith, *The Secret Gospel: The Discovery and Interpretation of the Secret Gospel According to Mark* (New York: Harper & Row, 1973); See also Helmut Koester, *Ancient Christian Gospels* (Philadelphia: Trinity Press International, 1990), 293–95.

37. Smith, *Jesus the Magician*, 16.

38. Ibid., chap. 6; Howard Clark Kee, *Miracle in the Early Christian World: A Study in Sociohistorical Method* (New Haven: Yale University Press, 1983), 257.

39. See Ramsay MacMullen, *Paganism in the Roman Empire* (New Haven, Conn.: Yale University Press, 1981).

40. A. E. Harvey, *Jesus and the Constraints of History* (Philadelphia: Westminster Press, 1982), 110, 113–14 .

41. In addition to *Jesus and Judaism*, see E. P. Sanders, *Jewish and Christian Self-Definition* (London: SCM Press, 1981), vol. 2; E. P. Sanders, *Paul, the Law, and the Jewish People* (Philadelphia: Fortress Press, 1983); E. P. Sanders, *Judaism, Practice and Belief 63 B.C.E.–66 C.E.* (London: SCM Press; Philadelphia: Trinity Press International, 1992).

42. Sanders, *Jesus and Judaism*, 18, 22.

43. Ibid., 4–5.

44. Ibid., 8, 11–12. See also E. P. Sanders, *The Historical Figure of Jesus* (London: Penguin Press, 1993), 94–95.

45. Sanders, *Jesus and Judaism*, 61, 63, 70–71.

46. Ibid., 71.

47. Ibid., 77, 87, 97.

48. Jacob Neusner, "Money-changers in the Temple: The Mishnah's Explanation," *New Testament Studies* 35, no. 2 (1989), 287–90.

49. Craig Evans, "Jesus' Action in the Temple: Cleansing or Portent of Destruction?" *Catholic Biblical Quarterly* 51 (April 1989): 239.

50. Craig Evans, "Jesus' Action in the Temple and Evidence of Corruption in the First-Century Temple," in *Society of Biblical Literature 1989 Seminar Papers*, ed. D. J. Lull (Atlanta: Scholars Press, 1989), 523.

51. Bruce Chilton, *The Temple of Jesus: His Sacrificial Program within a Cultural History of Sacrifice* (University Park, Pa.: Pennsylvania State University Press, 1992), 111.

52. George Wesley Buchanan, "Symbolic Money-changers in the Temple?" *New Testament Studies* 37 (April 1991): 282.

53. David Seeley, "Jesus' Temple Act," *Catholic Biblical Quarterly* 55 (April 1993): 278–79.

54. Robert Miller, "The (A)historicity of Jesus' Temple Demonstration: A Test Case in Methodology," in *Society of Biblical Literature 1991 Seminar Papers,* ed. D. J. Lull (Atlanta: Scholars Press, 1991), 235–52.

55. Chilton, *Temple of Jesus*, 99.

56. Sanders, *Jesus and Judaism*, 264.

57. Ibid., 11.

58. Sanders, *Historical Figure of Jesus*, 94–95. The emphasis is Sanders's.

59. See also Sanders, *Jesus and Judaism*, 93: "It seems to be shared by the entirety of the early Christian movement."

60. E. P. Sanders and Margaret Davies, *Studying the Synoptic Gospels* (London: SCM Press, 1989), 16.

61. Sanders, *Historical Figure of Jesus*, 64.

62. Marcus Borg, *Jesus, A New Vision: Spirit, Culture, and Life of Discipleship* (San Francisco: Harper & Row, 1987), 15.

63. Ibid., 32, 43.

64. Ibid., 41.

65. Marcus Borg, *Conflict, Holiness and Politics in the Teachings of Jesus* (New York: Edwin Mellen Press, 1984), 86–87. See also Marcus Borg, *Jesus in Contemporary Scholarship* (Valley Forge, Pa.: Trinity Press International, 1994), chap. 5.

66. Borg, *Conflict, Holiness and Politics*, 131.

67. See also John Dominic Crossan, *In Fragments: The Aphorisms of Jesus* (San Francisco: Harper & Row, 1983); Robert C. Tannehill, *The Sword of His Mouth* (Philadelphia: Fortress Press; Missoula, Mont.: Scholars Press, 1975); Elisabeth Schüssler Fiorenza, *In Memory of Her: A Feminist Theological Reconstruction of Christian Origins* (New York: Crossroad, 1983).

68. See Marcus Borg, "An Orthodoxy Reconsidered: The 'End-of-the-World' Jesus," in *The Glory of Christ in the New Testament*, ed. L. D. Hurst and N. T. Wright (Oxford: Clarendon Press, 1987), 207–17; Borg, "Renaissance in Jesus Studies."

69. See Marcus Borg, "A Temperate Case for a Non-eschatological Jesus," *Forum* 2 (1986): 81–102; Borg, *Jesus in Contemporary Scholarship*, chap. 3.

70. Helmut Koester, "Jesus the Victim," *Journal of Biblical Literature* 111 (Spring 1992): 6.

71. Sanders, *Historical Figure of Jesus*, 180.

72. See Perrin, *Rediscovering the Teaching of Jesus*; Perrin, *Jesus and the Language of the Kingdom*.

73. Douglas R. A. Hare, *The Son of Man Tradition* (Minneapolis: Fortress Press, 1990).

74. Dodd, *Parables of the Kingdom*; Perrin, *Jesus and the Language of the Kingdom* (Philadelphia: Fortress Press, 1981).

75. Crossan, *Historical Jesus*, xxviii–xxix.

76. See Bernard Brandon Scott, "To Impose is Not/To Discover: Methodology in John Dominic Crossan's *The Historical Jesus*," in *Jesus and Faith: A Conversation on the Work of John Dominic Crossan*, ed. Jeffrey Carlson and Robert A. Ludwig (New York: Orbis Books, 1994), 22–30.

77. Crossan, *Historical Jesus*, 427–34.

78. Crossan, *Historical Jesus*, xxxiii.

79. See John Dominic Crossan, *The Cross That Spoke: The Origins of the Passion Narrative* (San Francisco: Harper & Row, 1988).

80. See Dale C. Allison, *Jesus of Nazareth: Millenarian Prophet* (Minneapolis: Fortress Press, 1998), 10–33.

81. John S. Kloppenborg, *The Formation of Q: Trajectories in Ancient Wisdom Collections* (Philadelphia: Fortress Press, 1987).

82. Steven Patterson, *The Gospel of Thomas and Jesus* (Sonoma, Calif.: Polebridge Press, 1993).

83. John P. Meier, *A Marginal Jew: Rethinking the Historical Jesus*, vol. 1, *The Roots of the Problem and Person* (Garden City, N.Y.: Doubleday, 1991), 125.

84. Francis T. Fallon and Ron Cameron, "The Gospel of Thomas: A Forschungsbericht and Analysis," *Aufstieg und Niedergang der romischen Welt* 25, no. 6 (1988): 4195–251.

85. Crossan, *Historical Jesus*, 243.

86. Walter J. Ong, *Orality and Literacy: The Technologizing of the Word*, ed. Terence Hawkes (London and New York: Methuen, 1982), 34.

87. See also John Dominic Crossan, *The Birth of Christianity: Discovering What Happened in the Years Immediately after the Execution of Jesus* (San Francisco: HarperSanFrancisco, 1998), 139–75.

88. See Richard Horsley, "Bandits, Messiahs, and Longshoremen: Popular Unrest in Galilee around the Time of Jesus," in *Society of Biblical Literature 1988 Seminar Papers* (Atlanta: Scholars Press, 1988), 194–99; Richard Horsley, *Jesus and the Spiral of Violence: Popular Jewish Resistance in Roman Palestine* (San Francisco: Harper & Row, 1987).

89. Crossan, *Historical Jesus*, 341; John Dominic Crossan, *Jesus: A Revolutionary Biography* (San Francisco: HarperSanFrancisco, 1994), 101.

90. Meier, *Marginal Jew*, 1: 7, 9.

91. See Hayden White, *The Content of the Form: Narrative Discourse and Historical Representation* (Baltimore: Johns Hopkins University Press, 1987).

92. See Julian V. Hills, "The Jewish Genius: Jesus According to John Meier," *Forum*, new series 1 (1998): 327–48.

93. Meier, *Marginal Jew*, 1:11.

94. Ibid., 168–77.

95. Ibid., 214.

96. Ibid., 221–22.

97. John P. Meier, *A Marginal Jew: Rethinking the Historical Jesus*, vol. 2, *Mentor, Message, and Miracles* (New York: Doubleday, 1994), 7, 35, 124.

98. Ibid., 265, 238.

99. Ibid., 241.

100. Ibid., 413 (Meier's translation), 423.

101. Ibid., 144, 453.

102. Ibid., 290.

103. N. T. Wright, *The New Testament and the People of God* (Minneapolis: Fortress Press, 1992), 45.

104. N. T. Wright, *Jesus and the Victory of God* (Minneapolis: Fortress Press, 1996), 138.

105. Ibid., 138.

106. Wright, *New Testament*, 45.

107. Ibid., 268–70.

108. Wright, *Jesus and the Victory of God*, 163, 207–8.

109. Ibid., 201, 190, 361.

110. Ibid., 340.

111. Ibid., 342–43, 348.

112. Ibid., 351, 358–59.

113. Ibid., 344, 362, 353–54.

114. Ibid., 362.

115. Ibid., 367.

116. Ibid., 359.

117. Robert W. Funk, *Honest to Jesus: Jesus for a New Millennium* (San Francisco: HarperSanFrancisco, 1996), 64.

118. Robert W. Funk, ed., *The Acts of Jesus: Search for the Authentic Deeds of Jesus* (San Francisco: HarperSanFrancisco, 1998).

119. Robert W. Funk and Roy W. Hoover et al. *The Five Gospels: The Search for the Authentic Words of Jesus* (New York: Macmillan, 1993), 35.

120. John Dominic Crossan, ed., *Foundations & Facets* (Philadelphia: Fortress Press, 1986).

121. Funk, *Acts of Jesus*, 36–37.

122. See Lane C. McGaughy, "Words before Deeds," *Forum*, new series 1 (1998) 387–98.

123. Scott, *Hear Then the Parables*.

124. Bernard Brandon Scott, "Essaying the Rock: The Authenticity of the Jesus Parable Tradition," *Forum* 2 (1986), 3–35.

125. Jeremias, *Parables of Jesus*, 24.

126. See Kloppenborg, *The Formation of Q*.

127. See Michael J. Wilkens and J. P. Moreland, eds., *Jesus under Fire: Modern Scholarship Reinvents the Historical Jesus* (Grand Rapids: Zondervan Publishing

House, 1995), especially Craig Blomberg, "Where Do We Start Studying Jesus?" 17–51; Ben Witherington III, *The Jesus Quest: The Third Search for the Jew of Nazareth* (Downers Grove, Ill.: InterVarsity Press, 1995); N. T. Wright, "Five Gospels but No Gospel: Jesus and the Seminar," in *Crisis in Christology: Essays in Quest of Resolution*, ed. William R. Farmer (Livonia, Mich.: Dove Booksellers, 1995).

128. See Luke Timothy Johnson, *The Real Jesus: The Misguided Quest for the Historical Jesus and the Truth of the Traditional Gospels* (San Francisco: HarperSanFrancisco, 1996).

129. Howard Clark Kee, "A Century of Quests for the Culturally Compatible Jesus," *Theology Today* 52 (April 1995): 17–28.

130. Robert J. Miller, *The Jesus Seminar and Its Critics* (Santa Rosa, Calif.: Polebridge Press, 1999).

131. Mark Allen Powell, *Jesus as a Figure in History* (Louisville, Ky.: Westminster John Knox Press, 1998), 81.

132. Allison, *Jesus of Nazareth*; Bart D. Ehrman, *Jesus: Apocalyptic Prophet of the New Millennium* (New York: Oxford University Press, 1999); Paula Fredriksen, *Jesus of Nazareth, King of the Jews: A Jewish Life and the Emergence of Christianity* (New York: Alfred A. Knopf, 1999).

133. Meier, *Marginal Jew*, 1:177.

134. Ben F. Meyer, *The Aims of Jesus* (London: SCM Press, 1979).

135. Brad H. Young, *Jesus and His Jewish Parables: Rediscovering the Roots of Jesus' Teaching* (New York: Paulist Press, 1989).

136. Bruce Chilton, *A Galilean Rabbi and His Bible: Jesus' Use of the Interpreted Scripture of His Time* (Wilmington, Del.: Michael Glazier, 1984); Bruce Chilton, *The Temple of Jesus: His Sacrificial Program within a Cultural History of Sacrifice* (University Park, Pa.: Pennsylvania State University Press, 1992).

137. See George Foot Moore, "Christian Writers on Judaism," *Harvard Theological Review* 14 (July 1921): 197–254.

138. Marcus J. Borg, *Meeting Jesus Again for the First Time: The Historical Jesus and the Heart of Contemporary Faith* (San Francisco: HarperSanFrancisco, 1994).

139. Sanders, *Jesus and Judaism*, 333–34.

140. Meier, *Marginal Jew*, 1:197.

141. See David Tracy, *The Analogical Imagination: Christian Theology and the Culture of Pluralism* (New York: Crossroad, 1981).

142. Crossan, *Jesus: A Revolutionary Biography*, 190.

143. John P. Meier, "Reflections on Jesus-of-History Research Today," in *Jesus' Jewishness*, ed. James H. Charlesworth (New York: Crossroad, 1991), 92.

144. Richard A. Horsley and Jonathan A. Draper, *Whoever Hears You Hears Me* (Harrisburg, PA: Trinity Press International, 1999).

145. Marcus J. Borg and N. T. Wright, *The Meaning of Jesus: Two Visions* (San Francisco: HarperSanFrancisco, 1999).

146. See Steven Patterson, *The God of Jesus: The Historical Jesus and the Search for Meaning* (Harrisburg, Pa.: Trinity Press International, 1998).

147. Schweitzer, *Quest of the Historical Jesus*, 2.

# 2. THE REAL JESUS
## The Challenge of Current Scholarship and the Truth of the Gospels
*Luke Timothy Johnson*

I got into the "Jesus Wars" only bit by bit and almost by accident, by writing reviews of books by John Bowden, Bishop Spong, John Dominic Crossan, and John Meier, and finally on the *Five Gospels*, the published result of the well-publicized Jesus Seminar's first five years of labor. I approached these books with some skepticism.[1] I was not convinced that the new quest for the historical Jesus in these and many other publications had any greater chances of success than the one described by Albert Schweitzer in his classic study, *The Quest of the Historical Jesus* (1906).

There had been in the meantime significant archaeological discoveries at Qumran and at Nag Hammadi, but most scholars considered these of limited value for the historical knowledge of Jesus. Also, historians had started using comparative models drawn from the social sciences, but such models still had to be applied to the same old fragmentary and fragile evidence. As for the academic exercise of "discovering" new sources within old ones and using them to describe hypothetical communities, I remained a firm skeptic.

Nothing in these books dissuaded me from my bias, so I made my reviews as dismissive as I could manage, suggesting that they represented a noisy tempest in a tiny teapot. Thinking that I had only done what any clear-thinking scholar given the same task would have done, I was shocked to discover that my review of Spong generated some remarkably hostile mail asserting that (a) Spong was the only alternative to pointy-headed fundamentalists, and that (b) I must therefore be a disaffected academic who had no care for the real needs of the church—presumably, the insights of Bishop Spong.

This response made me realize that ordinary people were taking what I considered the shoddiest sort of scholarship as the real stuff. I saw that the flood of historical Jesus books written between 1990 and 1994 (not only by Crossan, who did four all by himself,[2] but also three by Marcus Borg,[3] and others by Barbara Thiering,[4] A. N. Wilson,[5] Steven Mitchell,[6] John Meier,[7] and of course, two by Bishop Spong[8]) and the constant stirring of the media pot by the Jesus Seminar between 1985 and 1995 was having a real impact on an American Christianity that was already in the most fragile possession of the classic Christian tradition and already deeply divided over the issue of how Christianity should engage the modern age.

Headlines connecting critical scholars with statements denying elements of the gospel story, together with the implication that if Jesus didn't say this, then Christians shouldn't believe it, had, I saw, two effects. For those lay people who retained some sense that scholars were in the truth business, such announcements created doubts about the church's confession. Even more disastrous, the many Christians who already thought that critical thought was a dangerous commodity for Christians took the careless declarations of the Jesus Seminar and the hype of the media as convincing proof that biblical scholars seek to undermine Christianity's claims. By forcing an artificial choice between scholarship and faith, these academics exacerbated an already grievous gap between religion and reason in our culture.

My interest in this essay is not to replace the various images of the historical Jesus offered by such publications with an alternative historical version that I consider superior to theirs. My title "The Real Jesus," in fact, is ironic, for it is a term carelessly invoked in these books. In contrast to the Jesus of Christian faith—understood as mythic and therefore untrue—they claim to offer the "real," that is, historical, Jesus. My reticence on this point does not stem from historical skepticism concerning Jesus. Just the opposite. I think that the historian can determine a number of extremely important things about Jesus as a human person within the first-century Mediterranean world. My point is rather that no historical reconstruction, however adequate, yields the "real Jesus."

I will not repeat here the detailed consideration of the Jesus Seminar and the various historical Jesus publications found in my book, *The*

*Real Jesus: The Misguided Quest for the Historical Jesus and the Truth of the Traditional Gospels,*[9] nor will I go into much of a cultural analysis, except to say that it is intriguing how publishers have marketed books on Jesus like books on Michael Jordan, and fascinating to see the Jesus Seminar's savvy manipulation of the media. Realizing that the American media covers only three things well—personalities, elections, and scandals—the Seminar cast its yearly performance in the form of an election (using colored beads) concerning a personality (Jesus) with just the hint of scandal (he was different than believers think). Instead, I want to focus on the fundamental misconceptions governing this effort and turn to the truth of the gospel (and the Gospels), which this errant contemporary quest misses completely.

When we compare the efforts of the Jesus Seminar and other recent historical Jesus books, we find that they share certain standard features:

(1) They start by rejecting the canonical Gospels as reliable sources for historical knowledge about Jesus. The Gospels of Matthew, Mark, Luke, and John must be purified of "later accretions" or the "distorting perspective of faith"; they must be supplemented by apocryphal writings, or alternatively, some more primitive and reliable source must be excavated from within them. In short, if the "real Jesus" is to be found, he must be found somewhere other than in the Gospels as they are read by Christians.

(2) They derive their portrait of Jesus without any reference to other canonical sources. In particular, they consider Paul's letters to be irrelevant to knowledge about Jesus. They see Paul as the inventor of the "Christ cult" that so many of them regard as the distortion of the pure "Jesus movement."

(3) They portray Jesus and his mission in terms of a social or cultural reform rather than in terms of religious or spiritual reality. Even Borg, who calls Jesus a charismatic figure, locates Jesus within Judaism by means of Jesus' criticism of its "politics of holiness" (a bad thing), which he replaces with the "politics of compassion" (a good thing).[10] For both Burton Mack and John Dominic Crossan, the Jesus movement was a cultural critique.[11] Crossan thinks that when the Jesus movement became Christianity, it had already lost its essential character. In their reconstructions, Jesus emerges as an egalitarian, multicultural,

nonjudgmental, nonauthoritarian critic of hierarchical and exclusionary institutions.

(4) Although calling themselves historical studies, these productions quickly expose a basically theological agenda. They consider traditional Christian belief as a distortion of the "real Jesus," and the Christian religion a distortion of what Jesus was really about. For Crossan and Mack, the destructive aspects of traditional Christianity are found not only in its developed creeds and institutions, but already within the narrative structures of the Gospels. They want their improved version of Jesus to reshape the cultural phenomenon called Christianity by removing what Mack calls "the privilege of Christian myth."[12]

(5) All these productions assume that historical knowledge is normative for faith and, therefore, for theology. Crossan states it succinctly: "If you cannot believe in something produced by reconstruction, you may have nothing left to believe in."[13] Connected to this is the assumption that origins define essence: the first understanding of Jesus (or Jesus' understanding of himself) must necessarily be more adequate than any later understanding, just as the original form of the Jesus movement was more authentic than any of its developments. In one way or another, they argue that a new understanding of historical Jesus should lead Christians to reject what Robert Funk calls the "theological tyranny" of the creeds that distort the "historical," that is, the "real" Jesus.[14]

There are many separate historiographical errors that can be identified in these publications. Take, for example, the Jesus Seminar's creation of criteria for authentic sayings of Jesus that guarantees the emergence of a certain image of Jesus. Or, take the Seminar's willingness to assert who Jesus "really was" when all it had yet considered was the sayings material of the Gospels and not the stories. Only slightly less baffling is Borg's basing his noneschatological Jesus on a poll of likeminded scholars, some 60 percent of whom agreed that Jesus did not predict the end of the world;[15] Crossan's rule of thumb that the more evidence there is that something has been interpreted, the less likely it is that it happened;[16] or Mack's detection of a phantom Q community's history through analysis of a phantom Q document.[17]

More troublesome is that historians should be so uncritical about their own craft, and, as a result, both distort its practice and bring it into discredit. In these remarks, I want to make clear, I exempt the sober and careful work of Father John Meier, whose two massive volumes promise to extend themselves into the largest historical Jesus project ever undertaken. I have separate difficulties with his venture, but he cannot be accused of historiographical charlatanism. Meier recognizes, for example, that the notion of a scientifically derived "historical Jesus" is scarcely unproblematic when studies over the past several decades, promising to deliver that historical figure and all using roughly the same methods and procedures, end up with such wildly divergent results as Jesus as the wicked priest from Qumran, as husband of Mary Magdalene and son of Sophia, as revolutionary zealot, as agrarian reformer, as revitalization movement founder, as guru of oceanic bliss, as gay magician, as cynic sage, as peasant thaumaturge, and as poet.

Apart from Meier, none of these authors deals with what history itself is about. It does not take much reflection to see that the notion of what is "historical" is not so obvious as they suppose. They use popular understandings of the historical rather than reflective ones. By their offer of a "historical Jesus," they also claim to render the "real Jesus," an equation that is manifestly false. History is simply not the same as reality.

History is a mode of human knowing, the application of critical intelligence to shared human memory. The history of any event or person is both less and more than a "real" person (if we can leave *that* tricky concept unexamined for a moment!). It is less because persons and events consist in much more than can possibly be filtered through perception, memory, record, and analysis. It is more because the very process of perception, memory, recording, and analysis is one in which the past is enriched by ever changing perspectives in the present.

What a fragmentary and fragile process is history! It is like a rough sieve that catches big chunks but lets a great deal of fine stuff through. To say that something is not historical, then, is not at all to say that it is not real. Fingernails are real but they are not properly historical; they escape the scan of human events in time and space. As for the lower end of existence, so for the upper: much of what we most value in human experience eludes historical knowing—alienation and reconciliation, forgiveness, hope, love, and compassion. If, then, we were to say that the resurrection of Jesus is not historical, it does not follow that it is not real. It simply opens up the question of what sort of reality the resurrection might be.

Historical knowing is not all knowing, nor historical truth all truth. Historical knowing is only one of the ways in which human intelligence apprehends reality. We can apprehend reality mathematically and through natural and social sciences, as well as through aesthetics and moral cognition. None of these ways of knowing is properly "historical," but it would be foolish on that count to deny them epistemological legitimacy. They are modes of knowledge, each of which, in its way, apprehends reality as adequately, if differently, than history does. Each mode also has its own criteria for what constitutes true knowing, which cannot be reduced to the criteria of historical knowledge.

There is an apprehension of reality and of human experience that is properly called religious, which can also make truth claims that can be tested according to its own criteria, which are also not those of history. To bring this home, it is possible for Christians to claim a knowledge of the "real Jesus" that is subject to the criteria of religious truth, but is not reducible to the categories of historiography.

Another example of conceptual confusion in historical Jesus research is the assumption that historical knowledge should be normative for Christian existence. For example, if it is discovered that Jesus did not claim to be the Messiah, Christians are mistaken in considering him so; if Jesus did not claim divinity, Christians wrongly attribute it to him.

Even a little reflection reveals how poor a premise this is, just in general. History does not by itself possess normative force. Take the recent American peacekeeping presence in Bosnia. Is it the lesson of Munich that demanded our soldiers be there? Or is it the lesson of Vietnam that should have kept us away? And what were the lessons of Munich and Vietnam, come to think of it? Historical lessons are more elusive than popular and political discourses suggest.

The decision by a community to treat something in its past as normative, furthermore, is not due to historical knowledge as such but to a much more complex apprehension of present experience, in which the record of the past is one among other factors. In 1950, for example, no British citizen would have denied that Winston Churchill was the savior of the nation. But that knowledge did not prevent the British from unceremoniously removing Churchill from the prime minister-ship at the earliest opportunity.

Trying to make a historically reconstituted Jesus the norm for con-temporary Christianity is in any case impossible. Reconstructions of any figure are always being revised, largely because they are usually not much more than distillates of a contemporary ethos and can never sus-tain the commitment of even a single person's life, much less the iden-tity of a community through time. In the case of Christianity, though, such reconstruction is strictly beside the point. Such efforts, to borrow a phrase from Paul's first letter to Timothy, "have missed the mark con-cerning the faith" (1 Tim 6:21).

The Christian creed does contain a number of historical assertions about Jesus. But Christian faith as a living religious response is not directed to those historical facts concerning a person of the past. And faith is certainly not directed to a historical reconstruction of that per-son. Christian faith responds to a living person. The "real Jesus" for Christian faith is the resurrected Jesus. The message to the women at the tomb in Luke 24:5 is precisely to the point: "Why are you seeking the Living One among dead people? He is not here, but has been raised." For Christian faith, the real Jesus is not simply "among the dead" but is supremely "among the living," indeed, "the living one."

Christians understand the resurrection to be not the resuscitation of Jesus' body to continue his former life, but as an empowerment that draws the human Jesus definitively into God's own way of existing. The resurrected Lord lives both in continuity with the human existence of Jesus (defined by space and time) and in discontinuity with it, for what-ever is meant by the resurrected body, it transcends the limitations of body and space which are defining for every other body we know. Jesus now has, in other words, a more powerful form of existence, which is mediated by the presence of the Holy Spirit among believers. The real Jesus for Christians is not simply a figure of the past but very much and above all a figure of the present, indeed, one who defines the present of believers by his presence.

From the beginning, Christians have taken the resurrection to be the defining event concerning Jesus and the fundamental perspective from which to assess the "real Jesus." It is not what Jesus said and did before his death that measures him, but what God did through Jesus after his death. From this perspective, whether Jesus during his lifetime declared himself Messiah or thought himself divine is quite irrelevant; by his resurrection, "God has made him both Messiah and Lord" (Acts 2:36), and he was "set apart as Son of God in power by the Spirit of Sanctification" (Rom 1:4). Whether Jesus predicted the parousia in his preaching is quite irrelevant; it is because he lives now as powerful Lord that the church expects him to inaugurate God's final triumph: "For since we believe that Jesus died and rose again, even so, through Jesus, God will bring with him those who have fallen asleep" (1 Thess 4:14).

Let me put it even more sharply. By all the criteria employed by the Jesus questers, the statement in Matt 18:20 fails to meet the requirements of authenticity. It is found in only one Gospel, and so fails the test of "multiple attestation." It is paralleled in the sayings of at least one rabbi, thus missing the crucial criterion of "dissimilarity." Finally, it is a statement that can be correlated more easily with themes in Matthew's Gospel (see especially 28:20) than with other "Jesus traditions," thus failing the test of "coherence."

Yet this statement, which historians cannot argue that Jesus said, is, in the view of Christian experience, most profoundly true: "For where two or three are gathered in my name, there am I in the midst of them." Perhaps he did say it. Does it matter? For Christians it is true, not as a statement about Jesus' past but as a statement about Jesus' life and presence in the present. We can also reverse the proposition. Suppose Jesus did say it, but there was no resurrection, no powerful presence experienced after his death. In what sense would the statement be "true" even if it were historical?

It is Jesus the risen Lord who is experienced in the assembly of believers, declared by the word of proclamation, encountered in the sacramental meal, addressed by prayers of praise and petition. It is "in the name" of this Jesus that powerful deeds are performed, that believers can express gifts of tongues and prophecy and teaching and service in the world, and it is by the spirit of freedom given by this same risen Lord that they are themselves transformed from glory to glory. So it was at the birth of the Christian religion. So it is today wherever Christianity is spiritually alive and identifiably Christian in character.

Historical Jesus research is irrelevant to Christian faith because the resurrection is not a historical but an eschatological event, indeed, a new creation. "The first human, Adam," Paul says, "became a living being. The second Adam became life-giving spirit" (1 Cor 15:45). "If anyone is in Christ," he says in another place, "there is a new creation" (2 Cor 5:17). By definition, Jesus' resurrection is inaccessible to historical knowing. Christians who declare, without shame or hesitation, that the resurrection is not historical, know that they are not denying the reality of the resurrection. They are rather insisting that a mode of knowing other than the historical is required to grasp it, the way of knowing that we call faith. The problem lies not in the reality of the resurrection, but in the limitations of history.

That quality of the Gospels the historical questers see as the hurdle to reaching the "real Jesus"—namely, their postresurrection perspective—Christians see as the truest thing about them. The questers say the real Jesus must be found in the facts of his life before his death. Christians say that the real Jesus is the one who is now alive and powerfully active in the lives of human persons. The Gospels provide access to the "real Jesus" precisely insofar as they reflect the perception of him given by his postresurrection existence.

From the perspective of Christian faith, the claim to capture the "real Jesus" anywhere short of his resurrection is as wrongheaded as a biography of Franklin Roosevelt that stopped at Campobello, or one of Churchill that ended before Dunkirk. What made these figures of our century historic—namely, their lives after crippling injury and political death—would by such a method be left out. It would be as misguided as my staying locked in my study, analyzing the records of my first date with my wife, trying to determine if she was really who she said, even while she vainly called to me from the other room, asking for some attention to her living presence.

There is still another way in which the present historical Jesus research is misguided. Participants seek the identity of Jesus. But they begin by dismantling the narrative framework of the Gospels as nonhistorical constructions of the postresurrection perspective. Then they take all the individual pieces of the Jesus tradition and pass them through the sieve of various criteria: multiple attestation, dissimilarity, coherence, and the rest. From the pile of the acceptable pieces, we are to suppose, will emerge the historical Jesus.

But nothing of the sort could ever emerge. A pile of filmclips does not make a movie. A collection of anecdotes does not constitute a novel. A set of discrete memories does not constitute an identity. Personal identity does not have to do with discrete events but with a meaningful pattern, a consistent character. Indeed, the subtler questers recognize that a pile of pieces does not provide its own coherence, so they import a pattern from outside the Gospels to give a new frame for the pieces: Jesus as revolutionary, Jesus as peasant, Jesus as charismatic.

What is not acknowledged is that the choice of the pattern has also affected the choice of the pieces; the pieces that fit the pattern are deemed authentic, those that do not are rejected. Thus is repeated the inevitable circularity that led Albert Schweitzer to observe that all historical Jesuses end up resembling their creators, and T. W. Manson to comment even more wryly, "By their Lives of Jesus ye shall know them."[18]

Some questers have in fact suggested that they are simply doing what the first Gospel writers were doing, that is, creatively fitting discrete memories to an interpretive pattern. Quite apart from the arrogant assumption of authority to rearrange the pieces, this procedure assumes that the first pattern, found in the canonical Gospels, is arbitrary, or erroneous, or harmful, so that in the light of a superior cultural level, a revised version is appropriate.

There are tremendous differences between the four canonical Gospels in terms of the facts of Jesus' ministry—differences that are real and a rebuke to anyone seeking to determine the precise sequence of Jesus' actions and words or to simply read the historical Jesus off the pages of these narratives. Despite that diversity, however, the four canonical Gospels—and only the canonical among all the so-called Gospels produced by the early Christian movement—share an identical and instantly recognizable pattern.

It is a pattern, however, that is found in the narratives as such. It is not determinable from one isolated statement or event, or any cumulative pile of such sayings and events. It is a narrative pattern that portrays an image of Jesus, his character, the character of his mission, and the character of discipleship. Since they are written from the perspective of the resurrection and of Jesus' powerful presence in the church, we might expect the image to be that of an all-powerful, triumphant, obviously divine figure whose transcendent attributes were in full and glittering display.

We know that this is not what we find. Rather, the identity of Jesus Christ as we find it in the four canonical Gospels is emphatically not that of a triumphant Lord. There are traces of that conviction, to be sure, in sayings, deeds, and moments of transfiguration. It is most obviously present in the Gospel of John. But the dominant image, constructed by the literary compositions of the Gospels themselves, is quite different.

We find it most starkly in Mark's Gospel, where the narrative focus is exclusively on the identity of Jesus and the drama of discipleship. Mark portrays Jesus above all as the suffering Son of man, who in obedience to God gives his life in service to all. And discipleship? It is not a present participation in glory, but a following in that messianic path of obedience and suffering service.

The Gospels of Matthew and Luke alter much in their Markan source and add substantial amounts of additional material, and so arrange the combination as to address their own ecclesial concerns. But this central image is not in the least eroded by Matthew or Luke. If anything, they intensify and extend the image of Jesus as the obedient servant of God. Most remarkably, the same image of Jesus and the same understanding of discipleship pervades the Gospel of John. Despite its fundamental reshaping of virtually every aspect of the gospel story—where Jesus was, how long he worked, how he talked, what deeds he did—John's grasp of Jesus' character and his portrayal of the character of discipleship is identical to that found in the other three Gospels.

Let me emphasize the basic point I am making. I agree that the Gospels are written from the perspective of resurrection faith even as they speak of Jesus' human life. But the image of the human Jesus they contain is a human image, not derivable from the conviction that he is now powerful Lord, nor reflective of that conviction. It is an image of human weakness, suffering, and service.

The question arises, is this narrative image simply a theological construction, perhaps invented by Mark? I would not be deeply disturbed by that proposition, for I believe the Holy Spirit led the early Christians into a deeper understanding of Jesus. And while we are at it, let us grant as well that the Holy Spirit's direction involved the reading of Jesus' life in terms of Torah. It was after the resurrection that his followers saw him in a new way because of their reading of the scriptures.

But is it correct to argue that the image of Jesus as the suffering servant is an arbitrary theological construction that just happened to infiltrate and dominate the other Jesus traditions? Or is the image of Jesus as the obedient and suffering servant the earliest communal memory of Jesus in the Church? Here we come to a decisive historiographical decision: Was the most accurate memory of Jesus in the Church that which concerned his sayings and his deeds, or was it that which concerned his character and the pattern of his life?

It is at this point, finally, where the truly irresponsible historical method of recent publications is most obvious. They systematically exclude Paul's letters from any consideration. This is irresponsible in the first place because Paul's letters—our very earliest extant Christian literature—contain statements confirming some ten aspects of Jesus' ministry and death, much as they are found in the canonical Gospels, compositions at least twenty years closer to Jesus' life. To ignore such evidence in favor of putative information derived by dubious methods from apocryphal writings composed between eighty and a hundred years after the canonical Gospels is simply inexcusable.

The real reason why the testimony of Paul is excluded is that Paul's letters also allude to the same narrative pattern concerning Jesus that we find in the canonical Gospels! Fundamental to Paul's teaching in several of his letters is an implied story of Jesus. Paul only rarely quotes the words of Jesus. He does not tell stories about Jesus. But he often evokes, alludes to, and applies the basic story of Jesus.

Paul's interest is not in the incidental details of Jesus' life: his Jewishness, his maleness, his itinerancy, or his speech patterns; these all belong to the irrecoverable past. But what Paul calls the *nous Christou*, the "mind of the Messiah," points to an outlook, a perception, a characteristic attitude, a pattern of behavior, a character that is Jesus' own and which can be replicated by the work of the Spirit in the lives of others. Paul can also refer to it as the *nomos Christou*, "the law of Christ," or perhaps better, "the pattern of the Messiah," which he spells out as "bearing one another's burdens."

Paul assumes the knowledge of this story pattern among his readers, even readers like those in the Roman church whom he had never met or taught. That Paul found the pattern of Jesus' self-sacrifice of first importance is obvious from the fact that one of his very few quotations from Jesus comes from his last meal with his disciples. Paul tells the Corinthians, "I also delivered to you, that the Lord Jesus on the night when he was betrayed took bread, and when he had given thanks, he broke it, and said, 'This is my body which is for you. Do this in remembrance of me.' In the same way also the cup, after supper, saying, 'This cup is the new covenant in my blood. Do this, as often as you drink it, in remembrance of me'" (1 Cor 11:23–25). This "memory" of Jesus is remarkably close to the synoptic accounts of the Last Supper.

Paul says that he did not himself invent these words but that he received them "from the Lord" (1 Cor 11:23). This citation of Jesus' words at the Last Supper is not an isolated occurrence. Paul alludes to the narrative pattern everywhere without any explanation, assuming that his readers would catch the allusion. He refers to Jesus as the one "who loved me and gave himself for me" (Gal 2:20; cf. 1:4; Eph 5:2; Titus 2:14), and to a member of the community as a "brother for whom Christ died" (1 Cor 8:11; Rom 14:15), and he exhorts his readers to "welcome one another as Christ has welcomed you" (Rom 15:7). He tells them to seek to build each other up rather than please only themselves: "For Christ did not please himself, but as it is written, 'the reproaches of those who reproach thee fell on me' [LXX Ps 68:9]" (Rom 15:2–3).

The pattern in Paul is the same as the one we find in the Gospels: Jesus is one who in faithful obedience to God gave his life in service to others. The fact that Paul can assume instant recognition of this pattern and its implications for life by his readers—even in churches not taught by him—within twenty years of the death of Jesus, argues strongly that the identity of Jesus found in the canonical Gospels is also the earliest normative memory of Jesus in the Church.

This, I submit, is the "real Jesus" apprehended by faith: a complex and mysterious combination of a present and powerful Lord whose spirit leads us through a path of service and suffering like his. It is an image of Jesus that is found in the writings of the New Testament as complete literary compositions available to every careful reader.

It is also an image of Jesus that is more profoundly countercultural and shocking to contemporary sensibilities than the Jesus purveyed by recent publications. At the end, I wonder whether the shocking and still scandalous implications of this image of Jesus are not what is most offensive to contemporary sensibilities even within the Church. I wonder whether this is not behind the scramble for an alternative Jesus better suited to an age of narcissism and self-esteem and political correctness. I wonder whether the quest for a Jesus who adjusts social arrangements is not also at the same time a flight from the Jesus who transforms the structures of human existence by the power of his Holy Spirit, and whose gift is also a call to follow in his path of suffering service to a suffering world.

NOTES

1. John Bowden, *Jesus: The Unanswered Questions* (Nashville: Abingdon Press, 1989); John Shelby Spong, *Born of a Woman: A Bishop Rethinks the Birth of Jesus* (San Francisco: HarperSanFrancisco, 1992) and *Resurrection: Myth or Reality?* (San Francisco: HarperSanFrancisco, 1994); John Dominic Crossan, *The Historical Jesus: The Life of a Mediterranean Jewish Peasant* (San Francisco: HarperSanFrancisco, 1991); John P. Meier, *A Marginal Jew: Rethinking the Historical Jesus*, vol. 1, *The Roots of the Problem and the Person* (New York: Doubleday, 1991) and vol. 2, *Mentor, Message, and Miracles* (New York: Doubleday, 1994); Robert W. Funk and Roy W. Hoover et al., *The Five Gospels: The Search for the Authentic Words of Jesus* (New York: Macmillan, 1993).

2. In addition to *The Historical Jesus* (noted above), John Dominic Crossan, *Jesus: A Revolutionary Biography* (San Francisco: HarperSanFrancisco, 1994); *The Essential Jesus* (San Francisco: HarperSanFrancisco, 1994); *Who Killed Jesus? Exposing the Roots of Anti-Semitism in the Gospel Story of the Death of Jesus* (San Francisco: HarperSanFrancisco, 1995).

3. Marcus J. Borg, *Jesus, A New Vision: Spirit, Culture, and the Life of Discipleship* (San Francisco: Harper & Row, 1987); *Meeting Jesus Again for the First Time: The Historical Jesus and the Heart of Contemporary Faith* (San Francisco: HarperSanFrancisco, 1994); Jesus in Contemporary Scholarship (Valley Forge, Pa.: Trinity Press International, 1994).

4. Barbara Thiering, *Jesus and the Riddle of the Dead Sea Scrolls: Unlocking the Secrets of His Life Story* (San Francisco: HarperSanFrancisco, 1992).

5. A. N. Wilson, *Jesus* (New York: W. W. Norton & Co., 1992).

6. Steven Mitchell, *The Gospel According to Jesus* (San Francisco: HarperSanFrancisco, 1991).

7. See note 1.

8. See note 1.

9. Luke Timothy Johnson, *The Real Jesus: The Misguided Quest for the Historical Jesus and the Truth of the Traditional Gospels* (San Francisco: HarperSanFrancisco, 1996).

10. Borg, *Jesus, A New Vision*, passim, esp. 131–49.

11. See Burton Mack, *The Lost Gospel: The Book of Q and Christian Origins* (San Francisco: HarperSanFrancisco, 1993); Crossan, *Historical Jesus*, esp. 303–53.

12. Mack, *Lost Gospel*, 254.

13. Crossan, *Historical Jesus*, 426.

14. Funk et al., *Five Gospels*, 7–8.

15. Borg, *Jesus, A New Vision*, 20, note 25.

16. Crossan, *Who Killed Jesus?* 82–117.

17. Mack, *Lost Gospel*.

18. T. W. Manson, "The Failure of Liberalism to Interpret the Bible as the Word of God," in *The Interpretation of the Bible,* ed. C. W. Dugmore (London: SPCK, 1944), 92.

# 3. RETRIEVING THE JEWISHNESS OF JESUS
## Recent Developments*

*Daniel J. Harrington, S. J.*

The Jewishness of Jesus has become a major topic among Christians and Jews. Some Christians still instinctively resist calling Jesus a Jew, and some Jews regard Jesus as an apostate who does not deserve to be called a Jew. But for many Christians and Jews, interest in the Jewishness of Jesus has been a positive and welcome development. It has enabled Christians to reclaim the humanity of Jesus and so to counter a longstanding temptation toward docetism (that is, the idea that Jesus only appeared to be human). Some Jewish writers have made serious efforts at bringing Jesus "home" by reclaiming him as a first-century Jew who stood for all the best in the Jewish tradition. The Second Vatican Council's call in 1965 for increased understanding between Catholics and Jews through biblical-theological study and dialogue has given official church encouragement to such undertakings.[1] And so the Jewishness of Jesus has engaged many Catholics, Protestants, and Jews for a large part of the second half of the twentieth century.

There is a certain level at which the Jewishness of Jesus is not controversial. Apart from the occasional fringe attempts to show that Jesus was born among the Gentile population of Palestine, or that Jesus never existed but was merely a mythic creation, there is no doubt that Jesus of Nazareth was born, lived, taught, and died as a Jew in the land of Israel in what we call the first century A.D.

Moreover, most of Jesus' teachings about God, creation, covenant, obedience to God's will, righteousness, and eschatology are consistent

---

* An earlier version of this article appeared in *New Theology Review* 11/2 (1998): 5–19.

with his Jewish theological heritage. Furthermore, the early Christian beliefs about Jesus—his relationship to God as Father, his identity, the significance of his life, the movement he began, his teachings about the coming kingdom of God, and his instructions about human attitudes and actions—use the language and concepts of Judaism. To say the same thing in other terms, Christian theology, Christology, soteriology, ecclesiology, eschatology, and ethics are rooted in Judaism. And we can say that through Jesus of Nazareth the great heritage of Judaism has been mediated to "all the nations" (Matt 28:19).

In my 1986 presidential address to the Catholic Biblical Association of America,[2] I tried to delineate three issues that had emerged in scholarly debates about the Jewishness of Jesus. These issues concerned the nature of Judaism in Jesus' time, the sources about Jesus the Jew, and our theological assessments about Jesus. Before moving on to four important developments during the last ten years, I want to review these three issues briefly because they remain unresolved.

The first issue was: What kind of Jew was Jesus? With the discovery of the Dead Sea Scrolls in the late 1940s and the restudy of other Jewish writings, it became clear that Judaism in Jesus' time was quite diverse socially and religiously. Thus, Jesus was understood in different ways on the basis of different literary sources: as an eschatological prophet on the basis of apocalyptic writings, as a political revolutionary on the basis of Josephus's reports about Jewish rebels against Rome, as an Essene on the basis of the Dead Sea Scrolls, as a Galilean charismatic on the basis of rabbinic descriptions of Galilean miracle-working rabbis, as a magician on the basis of Greek magical papyri, and so forth. The problem here was that our increased understanding of the diversity within Judaism in Jesus' time made it even more difficult to know precisely what kind of Jew Jesus was and against which Jewish background we should try to interpret him.

The second issue concerned the sources about Jesus and the method used to gain information about Jesus from them. The Jewish sources about Jesus are late and polemical (Talmudic passages, the *Toledot Jeshu* traditions) or suspect with regard to possible Christian influence (Josephus, *Ant.* 18:63–64). The Christian Gospels reflect a complicated process of transmission—from Jesus through the early communities to the Gospel texts written by the Evangelists—that took place over sixty or seventy years. Using the criterion of dissimilarity (what is dissimilar to Judaism [and early Christianity] can be attributed to Jesus), Christian scholars tended to take Jesus out of his Jewish context and make him discontinuous with Judaism. Using the criterion of similarity (what fits with Judaism can be attributed to Jesus), Jews (and some Christian scholars) contended that Jesus remained within the boundaries of Judaism.

The third issue concerns our theological assessments of Jesus. For Jews seeking to bring Jesus "home," Jesus was a Jewish teacher and in the end another victim of Roman oppression. For Christians, Jesus is that but much more. Christians regard Jesus as the agent of God, the authoritative interpreter of the Torah, whose death brought about the possibility of right relationship with God. We use terms such as redemption, reconciliation, justification, and atonement to express what happened as the result of Jesus' death and resurrection. The problem here is that however much Jews and Christians agree about Jesus, their ultimate theological assessments differ dramatically.

In this essay I want to take account of four scholarly developments regarding the Jewishness of Jesus that have interested me during the last ten years. The four issues concern the Dead Sea Scrolls, Jesus and wisdom, the death of Jesus, and Matthew and Judaism. In each case I want to outline the points of controversy and try to say what is at stake for Christians and Jews who are seriously pursuing the Jewishness of Jesus.

### The Dead Sea Scrolls

In the late 1980s and early 1990s the Dead Sea Scrolls became hot news again.[3] The slow pace of the official publication project (*Discoveries in the Judean Desert*) led some to take actions that would break what they regarded as the scholarly monopoly surrounding these texts. After some unpublished texts were reconstructed by computer from the Qumran concordance made in the 1950s, photographs of all the texts were made available to the general public in 1991.

The release of these texts was accompanied by some extreme and even bizarre claims about the Dead Sea Scrolls and their relevance for early Christianity. Michael Baigent and Richard Leigh claimed that the Qumran scrolls contain material that is embarrassing and even fatal to the traditional claims of Christianity, and that the Vatican had conducted a plot to suppress their publication.[4] Robert Eisenman maintained that the Qumran scrolls came from "the messianic movement" in Palestine that included Palestinian or "Jamesian" Christianity, and proceeded to find in them references to James, Jesus, and Paul.[5] Using what she called the "pesher method," Barbara Thiering claimed to find in the Qumran scrolls evidence that Jesus was part of the royal priestly line of the Qumran sect, was born out of wedlock, performed no miracles, did not die on the cross but was drugged and later revived in his burial cave, married twice, and fathered three children.[6]

In the face of such claims masquerading as scholarship and eagerly repeated in the popular media, it is easy for serious religious people to write off the recent controversies about the Dead Sea Scrolls as media sensationalism. There are, however, two developments that especially deserve the attention of Christians and Jews who are interested in the Jewishness of Jesus: the newly available texts that provide parallels to the Gospels, and the place of the Qumran scrolls within second temple Judaism and their significance for our understanding of Judaism in Jesus' time and its relation to early Christianity.

The claim that Qumran Cave 7 contained fragments of the Greek New Testament (and in particular that 7Q5 can only be Mark 6:52–53) remains dubious, despite efforts at reviving the hypothesis.[7] Likewise, it is very difficult to prove the direct influence of the Dead Sea Scrolls on the New Testament books. The most common scholarly view, which I share, is that the Dead Sea Scrolls and the New Testament represent independent and roughly contemporary Jewish movements. And so they provide parallels.

I want to focus here on three parallels between newly available Qumran texts and Gospel passages. The Aramaic "Son of God" text (4Q246) describes someone in these terms: "The Son of God he will be proclaimed, and the Son of the Most High they will call him." This sounds very much like Luke 1:32, 35: "He will be called the Son of the Most High. . . . [H]e will be called the Son of God." The problem is the fragmentary nature of the Qumran text and the difficulty involved in identifying the character about whom these claims were made. The many allusions to Daniel 7 suggest an eschatological scenario and point to a messianic figure who will merit the titles "Son of God" and "Son of the Most High." However, it is also possible to interpret the text negatively as an attack on the divine pretensions of such historical figures as Antiochus IV Epiphanes or Alexander Balas.

According to John 19:37, the soldier who pierced Jesus' side to make sure that he was dead ironically fulfilled Zech 12:10: "They will look on the one whom they have pierced." Some scholars have found the idea of a "pierced" messiah in 4Q285, a text based on the messianic language in Isa 10:34 and 11:1 ("a shoot from the stump of Jesse . . . the Branch of David"). The Qumran text contains the Hebrew verb *hmytw* that can conceivably be read with "Branch of David" as the subject ("he will kill him") or as the object ("they will kill him"). The context of Isa 11:1 and Hebrew grammar strongly favor the former reading. But if the latter reading ("they will kill him") is followed, then 4Q285 would provide evidence for the motif of the suffering or "pierced" messiah in the Dead Sea Scrolls.

In response to emissaries from John the Baptist in Matt 11:5/Luke 7:22, Jesus replies: "Go and tell John what you hear and see: the blind receive their sight, the lame walk, the lepers are cleansed, the deaf hear, the dead are raised, and the poor have the good news brought to them." This is the language of Isa 35:5–6 and 61:1—except for the clause "the dead are raised." A Qumran text (4Q521), which is clearly dependent on the same biblical passages, reads as follows: "He who liberates the captives, restores sight to the blind, straightens the bent . . . will heal the wounded and revive the dead, and bring good news to the poor." What is striking is the inclusion of "revive the dead" as in the Gospel passages. The texts of 4Q521 and Matt 11:5/Luke 7:22 agree against their sources in Isaiah in their including mention of resurrection. But the problem again is the fragmentary nature of the Qumran text and the ambiguity of its main character. Whereas the Gospel texts clearly describe the works of Jesus the Messiah, the Qumran text probably refers to God rather than to a messianic figure.

What significance do these three parallels have for the Jewishness of Jesus? On the one hand, their fragmentary character and ambiguity preclude definitive interpretations along messianic/christological lines. On the other hand, if we allow the maximalist interpretations—Son of God and Son of the Most High as messianic titles, the "pierced" messiah, and resurrection of the dead as a work of the messiah—then we encounter some very important questions: To what extent were the language and conceptuality applied to Jesus in the New Testament already part of pre-Christian Judaism? Were the early Christians attributing to Jesus terms and motifs already familiar in second temple Jewish circles?

Very early in the study of the Qumran scrolls the group behind the texts was identified as Essene and regarded as a Jewish sect. It was assumed that apart from the biblical texts and some other writings, most of the Qumran manuscripts were sectarian compositions. In recent years these positions have been questioned. Though the Essene hypothesis remains plausible, the affinity with certain positions called "Sadducean" in later Jewish sources raises questions about the extent to which the Qumran scrolls represent a major movement (and not just a sect) in second temple Judaism. Likewise, the corpus of "sectarian" documents has grown smaller through the years, and been reduced by some to the *Community Rule, Hodayot,* and *Habakkuk Pesher.*

Without embracing the extreme theories of Robert Eisenman about "the Jewish messianic movement"[8] or the equally extreme theory of Norman Golb that the Qumran library was moved from Jerusalem shortly before A.D. 70 and therefore had little or no intrinsic relation to the archaeological site at Qumran and the people who lived there,[9] one can legitimately raise questions about the extent of the religious movement behind the Qumran scrolls. Are the Qumran scrolls evidence for a small Jewish sect only, or for a major movement within second temple Judaism? If the latter, can this provide the proper background for studying the Jewishness of Jesus?

These are big questions to hang on fragmentary and often ambiguous texts. But for those interested in the Jewishness of Jesus, the newly available Qumran texts drive us back to some basic issues: the origin of early Christian terminology about Jesus, and the origin of the Jewish movement that became the Christian Church.

## Jesus and Wisdom

Recent biblical scholarship has shown a lively interest in Jesus as a Jewish wisdom teacher.[10] The teachings attributed to Jesus in the synoptic Gospels often take the literary forms used by other Jewish wisdom teachers in antiquity: proverbs, beatitudes, parables, rhetorical questions, admonitions, instructions, and so forth. Several sayings in the synoptic tradition present Jesus as the agent or emissary of divine wisdom (see Luke 7:35; 11:49–50), while others appear to identify Jesus as the Wisdom of God incarnate (see Luke 10:22/Matt 11:27; Luke 13:34/Matt 23:37).

Three of the earliest Christian hymns preserved in the New Testament celebrate Jesus as the Wisdom of God. Colossians 1:15–20 describes Jesus as "the image of the invisible God, the firstborn of all creation" and treats Jesus' role in creation in terms of what earlier Jewish wisdom texts (Proverbs 8, Sirach 24) say about the figure of Wis. The author of Hebrews affirms Jesus' superiority as Son of God over the angels by identifying him as Wisdom in terms reminiscent of Wisdom 7: "He is the reflection of God's glory and the exact imprint of God's very being, and he sustains all things by his powerful word" (Heb 1:3).

The most famous wisdom text in the New Testament is the Prologue to John's Gospel: "In the beginning was the Word . . ." (John 1:1–18). The Word is God's Wisdom. As such, the Word was in the beginning, had a role in creation, and came into the history of God's people. John's Prologue, however, goes beyond those texts by asserting that in Jesus of Nazareth the Wisdom of God took on human form: "The Word became flesh and lived among us" (1:14).

That Jesus was at least in part a Jewish wisdom teacher, that he regarded himself (or was regarded) as the agent of divine Wisdom, and that early Christians celebrated him as the Wisdom of God are important positive contributions to our appreciation of the Jewishness of Jesus. As a teacher, Jesus used the literary forms and the content of Jewish wisdom. And his identity as a Jewish wisdom teacher was appreciated and celebrated in terms and motifs already familiar to Jews and Jewish Christians from the texts about Wisdom as a personal figure.

Interest in Jesus as a Jewish wisdom teacher has important implications for those concerned with the Jewishness of Jesus. The Jewish wisdom books were originally part of the larger international wisdom movement in the ancient Near East. Likewise, in the present, the Jewish wisdom books and the wisdom teachings of Jesus can serve as a bridge or common ground for dialogue between Jews and Christians, and between them and representatives of other religious traditions. The concerns of wisdom literature—how to choose friends, how to avoid trouble, how to be happy, and so forth—are universal. As such, these wisdom teachings can facilitate the mutual understanding and respect that are the goals of interreligious dialogue.

The understanding of Jesus as Wisdom personified and incarnate has great significance also for Christology. The Jewish wisdom hymns portray the figure of Wisdom with feminine characteristics. This may be due merely to the fact that in both Hebrew and Greek the words for "wisdom"—*hokma* and *sophia*—are feminine in gender. There may, however, be deeper roots in the history of religions (the Mother Goddess, Isis, or some other figures) and in human psychology. What is striking is that early Christians could apply to Jesus of Nazareth the feminine imagery traditionally attached in Judaism to Wisdom personified. This in turn suggests that Jesus as the Wisdom of God represents both genders of humankind, and that we can and should move beyond androcentrism in our Christology and theology.

Scholarly interest in Jesus and wisdom has also been responsible for lively controversies concerning the sayings source Q and the historical Jesus. The sayings source Q is the collection of Jesus' sayings that is supposed to have been used independently by Matthew and Luke to supplement the rather sparse teaching material included in Mark's Gospel. Though we do not possess the manuscript of Q, many biblical scholars believe that the text can be reconstructed from the parallels in Matthew and Luke.

What emerges from this reconstruction is a mixture of wisdom and eschatology. Especially controversial in recent Q scholarship have been attempts at separating the wisdom and eschatological strata, and at writing the history of the Q community in light of this literary stratification.[11] The earliest stratum of Q appears in this analysis to have been a wisdom instruction like those in Proverbs 1–9 and 22–24 and in

Sirach. The content of the Q wisdom instruction can be found chiefly in Luke's Sermon on the Plain (6:20–49) and in teachings presented throughout Luke 9–14, and their parallels in Matthew. The topics include true happiness, love of enemies, avoiding hypocrisy, the relation between words and deeds, the simple lifestyle, confidence in God's care, dealing with anxiety, the kingdom of God, and discipleship.

In form and content, the early wisdom instruction extricated from Q appears mainly at home within Judaism. The methodological problem is whether one can or should separate sapiential and eschatological elements in a first-century Jewish wisdom instruction, since the Qumran wisdom writings and related texts freely join such elements. Even more dubious is the attempt to move from the dissection of a reconstruction of a hypothetical text to the historical description of phases in an early Christian movement.

Some researchers have suggested that the Jesus of the Q wisdom stratum looks like a Cynic philosopher, a relatively common figure in the Greco-Roman world (of which the land of Israel was part).[12] The major themes and the ironic tone of the Q wisdom stratum fit with the concerns and style of Cynic philosophers. In such a setting, "kingdom of God" might refer not to the future, cosmic intervention of God described in Jewish apocalyptic texts, but rather to that sphere of human nature or history that is beyond or superior to all human rulers. Although the "Jesus as Cynic" approach does not necessarily deny the Jewishness of Jesus, it does tend at least to make him less distinctively a Palestinian Jew and more closely allied to non-Jewish figures and movements in the Greco-Roman world.

At this point we are in a realm filled with hypotheses. But if we can reconstruct the text of Q, if we can arrive at a wisdom instruction as the earliest stratum of Q, if we can get behind to the Q community, perhaps we can reconstruct the actual teachings of the historical Jesus. This is the project of the Jesus Seminar. Using the Q sayings and noncanonical Gospels such as the Gospel of Thomas, the Jesus Seminar has tried to distinguish those sayings that may well come from Jesus from those that could conceivably, probably do not, and definitely do not come from Jesus.[13] The results are sparse. Jesus emerges not so much as a

Jewish wisdom teacher but rather as a somewhat de-Judaized professor of religious studies who says witty but mysterious things, is full of irony and paradox, and is ultimately harmless—not the kind of person likely to have been crucified by the Roman officials in Palestine.

## The Death of Jesus

The official creed of the Christian Church states that Jesus "suffered under Pontius Pilate, was crucified, died, and was buried." What is perhaps the earliest credal statement of all (1 Cor 15:3–5) says "that Christ died for our sins in accordance with the Scriptures, and that he was buried." There can be no doubt about the central significance of Jesus' death and resurrection for Christian faith from the beginning.

Two questions regarding Jesus' death have especially concerned New Testament scholars during the past decade: Why was Jesus put to death? Who was responsible for his death?

Those who focus on the wisdom teachings of Jesus in Q or who present him as resembling a Cynic philosopher have a hard time explaining what got Jesus killed. The material seems too generic and mysterious to warrant the vigorous response that issued in Jesus' death on the cross.

A more promising approach to what got Jesus killed is E. P. Sanders's understanding of Jesus as an eschatological charismatic and a herald of Israel's national restoration. According to Sanders, Jesus viewed himself as God's last messenger before the establishment of God's kingdom. His action at the Jerusalem temple (see Mark 11:15–19) was intended as a prophetic demonstration, a symbolic action calling for a renewed Israel. This prophetic action, however, was interpreted as potentially revolutionary by Roman and Jewish officials. And so Jesus was executed under the Roman prefect, Pontius Pilate, at the behest of Jewish leaders (including at least the high priests). The fact that Jesus' disciples were not also rounded up and executed implies that Pilate did not consider them and Jesus much of a threat.[14]

There is much that is persuasive in Sanders's approach. Placing the death sentence passed on Jesus in relation to his temple action follows the lead of the Evangelists (see Mark 14:57–58; Matt 26:60–61). Moreover, the cooperation between Pilate and the Jewish officials is historically plausible. It was in the interest of both to keep the peace in Jerusalem during Passover. The basic problem with Sanders's view is that Jesus' execution appears to have been a tragic mistake rather than the direct consequence of his life and teaching. According to Sanders, the kingdom proclaimed by Jesus was to be otherworldly in origin, one brought about by God and not by military insurrection. Then God would step in and provide a new temple, a restored people of Israel, and a renewed social order in which sinners have a place. By arresting and executing Jesus, Pilate and the Jewish leaders mistook a relatively harmless religious visionary for a political revolutionary.

Latin American liberation theologian Jon Sobrino regards Jesus' death on the cross not as a tragic mistake but rather as the natural and necessary consequence of his life and teaching. Here Sobrino follows the perspective of the Evangelists. They say that Jesus was almost universally misunderstood and rejected precisely because his life and teaching posed a radical threat to political and religious powers. Jesus died because he got in the way of those who wanted to protect their political and religious power. Thus, there was a continuity between Jesus' life of service for others and his death on the cross. Sobrino also finds a continuity between the Suffering Servant of Isaiah 53, Jesus' death on the cross, and the crucified peoples today who bear witness to God's kingdom.[15]

In a more historical vein, N. T. Wright regards the death of Jesus as the consequence of who Jesus thought he was and what he did. According to Wright, Jesus was conscious of a vocation, given by the one whom he knew as Father, to enact in himself what in Israel's Scriptures God had promised to accomplish all by himself—the returning and redeeming action of the covenant God. Wright's Jesus is very much an eschatological prophet who proclaims God's kingdom by rooting it in Israel's story. The major elements in this story are the return from exile, the defeat of evil and rescue of God's people, and the return of YHWH to Zion. Fidelity to his vocation led to Jesus' death at the hands of the powers that be—the Romans and their Jewish collaborators who were interested in preserving the status quo.[16]

This debate about the historical reason for Jesus' death has implications for the Jewishness of Jesus. What distinguished Jesus' death from those of Maccabean martyrs, the "social bandits" described by Josephus during Jesus' own time, or even the victims of the Holocaust in the twentieth century? Jesus of Nazareth was not the only first-century Jew who represented a radical threat to the political and religious powers of his day. Why did the death of this Jew become so important?

The debate about the historical reason for Jesus' death moves naturally into a second issue: the historical responsibility for Jesus' death. That the ultimate legal responsibility lay with the Roman prefect, Pontius Pilate, is indicated by several factors. Crucifixion was the Roman form of capital punishment for rebels and slaves, whereas Jews used stoning. Pilate had the judicial authority to inflict capital punishment, whereas Jews at this time probably did not. The official charge against Jesus was "King of the Jews," which sounds like a Roman political translation of the Jewish term "messiah."

If Pilate bore the ultimate legal responsibility for Jesus' death, it is also true that the Evangelists tended to decrease Pilate's responsibility and to increase that of the Jewish leaders and even the Jewish people as a whole (see Matt 27:25). The historical question is: How responsible were they?

There was a vigorous debate on this question over thirty years ago. That debate included the extreme positions of no Jewish responsibility[17] and extensive Jewish responsibility (following the Evangelists), with most scholars (Jews and Christians) coming to the position of some secondary Jewish responsibility but not nearly as much as the Gospels suggest. Of course, whatever Jewish responsibility there was historically involved only the high priests and their allies, not all Jerusalem or the entire Jewish people in Jesus' time (despite Matt 27:25) or the Jewish people throughout the ages.

After a fairly long hiatus, the debate about Jewish responsibility for Jesus' death revived in recent years in connection with Raymond E. Brown's *The Death of the Messiah*. Brown's primary goal was "to explain in detail what the Evangelists intended and conveyed to their audiences by their narratives of the passion and death of Jesus."[18] Brown also tried at many points to delineate what historical events might lay behind the

New Testament passion narratives. He recognized fully and demonstrated convincingly that these texts freely join historical information, fulfillment of biblical texts, and Christian theology.

Brown was challenged vigorously by John Dominic Crossan in his book *Who Killed Jesus?* Crossan admitted the merit of Brown's work: "His commentary is massive, monumental, and magisterial, and will be used as an encyclopedia of basic reference well into the next millennium."[19] Crossan's quarrel was with Brown's attempts at treating the Gospel passion narratives as historical sources. He describes Brown's approach as "history remembered" in that it assumes that a good amount of history can be retrieved from the passion narratives.

The subtitle of Crossan's work, *Exploring the Roots of Anti-Semitism in the Gospel Story of the Death of Jesus*, expressed one of his special concerns. He contends that the Gospels' stress on Jewish responsibility for Jesus' death and on Roman innocence, however understandable it may have been in the first century C.E., became a powerful vehicle for the growth of anti-Judaism and the subsequent development of European anti-Semitism. Crossan regards the belief that the Jews killed Jesus as an early Christian myth directed against rival Jewish groups but without historical foundation. He describes its repetition as "the longest lie" and contends that it must be eradicated from authentic Christian faith.

For those interested in the Jewishness of Jesus, this debate about Jewish responsibility for Jesus' death and the nature of the passion narratives has obvious importance. My own scholarly sympathies are with Brown. I think that some historical information can be recovered from analysis of the passion narratives and that they cannot be explained as mainly the result of early Christian midrash (a combination of biblical interpretation and religious imagination). But I also think (as does Brown) that Christians are obliged to face up to the tendency in the Gospels to blame Jews and exculpate Romans for Jesus' death. And I contend that both Jews and Christians today need to approach this matter with a sense of history, especially with regard to how Christians and Jews related to each other in the late first century when the Gospels were being composed.

## Matthew and Judaism

It is often said that Matthew is the most Jewish Gospel. It begins with a genealogy that roots Jesus in Israel's history from Abraham through David and the Babylonian exile up to Joseph and Mary. It makes frequent appeals to Old Testament fulfillment quotations: "All this took place to fulfill what had been spoken by the Lord through the prophet" (1:22). It presupposes knowledge of Jewish history and customs, and the Matthean Jesus often involves himself in debate about Jewish practices.

It is also often said that Matthew is the most anti-Jewish Gospel. It speaks frequently in negative contexts about "their synagogues" and warns against the hypocrisy of scribes and Pharisees. Its attack against the Jewish spiritual leaders in chapter 23 paints a picture of legalism and bad faith. It alone contains the people's self-curse as Pilate sentences Jesus to death: "His blood be on us and on our children" (27:25). Since Matthew has been historically the most influential Gospel, its apparent anti-Judaism has contributed greatly to the anti-Semitism that has marked subsequent Christian history.

How then can Matthew's Gospel be both Jewish and anti-Jewish? This paradox is best explained, I believe, by placing the Gospel in its original historical setting. An important development over the past decade or so has been the effort to read Matthew within the crisis that faced all Jews after the destruction of the Jerusalem temple in A.D. 70. In this context, Matthew's Gospel is one among several Jewish responses to a most traumatic event in Jewish history.

Matthew's Gospel was apparently composed around A.D. 85–90 in Greek in a city with a large Greek-speaking Jewish population. The most likely places are Antioch in Syria, Damascus, and Caesarea Maritima in Palestine. Matthew's Gospel is generally viewed as a revised and expanded edition of Mark's Gospel on the basis of Q and other traditions. It tried to explain how the heritage of Judaism could be carried on after A.D. 70—after the temple had been destroyed and Jews had even less political power in the land of Israel.

This crisis elicited various responses among Jews in the late first century. The political rebels went underground and prepared to regroup their forces during the Second Jewish Revolt under Simon bar Kokhba

(A.D. 132–135). The apocalyptists (in the tradition of the book of Daniel) counseled patience and trust in God's promises. And so the Jewish apocalypses known as 4 Ezra and 2 Baruch combine hope for God's dramatic intervention in the future with faithful observance of the Torah in the present. A third, and ultimately more influential, response has been called "formative Judaism"—the combination of priestly, scribal, and Pharisaic traditions that later issued in what is known as rabbinic Judaism.[20]

In this historical context, the Jewish features of Matthew's Gospel become intelligible. With his genealogy, fulfillment quotations, and other Jewish elements, Matthew sought to show that the great heritage of Judaism is best carried on among those who gather around Jesus as Lord and take him as the authoritative interpreter of the Torah. The five great speeches in Matthew's Gospel (chaps. 5–7, 10, 13, 18, 24–25) provide ample content for those who wish to follow the way of Jesus. And Jesus' death on the cross took place "according to the scriptures," especially Psalm 22—the psalm of the righteous sufferer.

In this context, the anti-Jewish features also become intelligible. The debate with representatives of "their synagogues"—most likely a symbol for formative Judaism—allowed Matthew to present Jesus' positions on controversial issues within late first-century Judaism: Sabbath observance (12:1–14), ritual purity (15:1–20), and marriage and divorce (19:1–9). In this context, the polemic against the scribes and Pharisees in chapter 23 takes on the appearance of an intense religious family feud, analogous to Christian controversies between Catholics and Protestants in the sixteenth century. In this context, the people's self-curse in Matt 27:25 becomes part of Matthew's conviction that Jewish rejection of Jesus was a factor in the Roman destruction of Jerusalem in A.D. 70. The text concerns not all Jews throughout the ages but rather those of Jesus' time and of the next generation ("on us and on our children").

Such a historical reading of Matthew's Gospel is well expressed in monographs by J. Andrew Overman and Anthony J. Saldarini. In *Matthew's Gospel and Formative Judaism* (1990), Overman argues that Matthew's Gospel should be read as reflecting the experience of a

Jewish-Christian community in competition and conflict with formative Judaism after the destruction of the temple in A.D. 70. Overman
states, "The struggle and eventual separation between formative and
Matthean Judaism have all the emotion and conflict of a family falling
apart."[21]

In *Matthew's Christian-Jewish Community* (1994), Saldarini contends that the Matthean group and its spokesperson (the Evangelist)
believed in Jesus as the Messiah and Son of God, still thought of themselves as Jews, and were still identified with the Jewish community by
others. Saldarini concludes that Matthew's Gospel originally addressed
"a deviant group within the Jewish community in greater Syria, a
reformist Jewish sect seeking influence and power (relatively unsuc-
cessfully) within the Jewish community as a whole."[22]

For those concerned with the Jewishness of Jesus, this attempt at
reading the most Jewish and anti-Jewish Gospel in the context of late
first-century Judaism has important implications. It makes more intelligible the Matthean insistence on the Jewish characteristics of Jesus
and of the movement he began. It also makes more intelligible the
harsh attacks directed against the rivals of Jesus—the representatives of
"their synagogues."

Even though Matthew's anti-Judaism may be intelligible in its first-
century context, that is of course no excuse for Christians to carry it
forward to the present. In this sense, historical study can and should be
liberating. There is no need to transfer a first-century religious family
feud within Judaism to the twentieth century. Whereas both funda-
mentalist and purely literary analyses prescind from the life-setting of
the text, historical analysis can help Christians and Jews to face their
past and to construct a different present and future.

### Conclusion

For those interested in retrieving the Jewishness of Jesus, the past
decade has brought some important developments and challenges.
First, the newly available Dead Sea Scrolls have raised questions about
the language used to describe Jesus in the New Testament and about the
origin of the Christian movement. Second, the recognition of Jesus as a

Jewish wisdom teacher has helped to explain why early Christian hymns celebrated him as the Wisdom of God. It has also fostered research on the earliest sources for Jesus' wisdom teachings and on his relation to Jewish and non-Jewish wisdom teachers. Third, renewed concern with Jesus' death has focused on whether it was a historical necessity or a tragic mistake, and on the extent to which we may follow the Gospels in attributing responsibility to the Jewish authorities. Fourth, reading Matthew's Gospel in the historical setting of the crisis facing all Jews in the late first century has helped to explain why it can be at once the most Jewish and most anti-Jewish Gospel.

## NOTES

1. Austin Flannery, ed., *Vatican II: The Conciliar and Post-Conciliar Documents* (Northport, N.Y.: Costello Publishing Co., 1975), 740–42.

2. Daniel J. Harrington, "The Jewishness of Jesus: Facing Some Problems," *Catholic Biblical Quarterly* 49 (January 1987): 1–13.

3. See Daniel J. Harrington, "What's New(s) about the Dead Sea Scrolls?" *Cross Currents* 44 (spring 1994–95): 463–75.

4. See Michael Baigent and Richard Leigh, *The Dead Sea Scrolls Deception* (New York: Summit Books, 1991).

5. See Robert Eisenman and Michael Wise, *The Dead Sea Scrolls Uncovered* (Shaftesbury, England: Element Press, 1992).

6. See Barbara Thiering, *Jesus and the Riddle of the Dead Sea Scrolls* (San Francisco: HarperSanFrancisco, 1992).

7. See Carsten P. Thiede, *The Earliest Gospel Manuscript?* (Exeter, England: Paternoster Press, 1992).

8. See Eisenman and Wise, *The Dead Sea Scrolls Uncovered.*

9. See Norman Golb, *Who Wrote the Dead Sea Scrolls?* (New York: Charles Scribner's Sons, 1995).

10. See Ben C. Witherington, *Jesus the Sage* (Minneapolis: Fortress Press, 1994).

11. See John S. Kloppenborg, *The Formation of Q* (Philadelphia: Fortress Press, 1987).

12. See John Dominic Crossan, *The Historical Jesus: The Life of a Mediterranean Jewish Peasant* (San Francisco: HarperSanFrancisco, 1991); F. Gerald Downing, *Cynics and Christian Origins* (Edinburgh: T. & W. Clark, 1992); and Burton L. Mack, *The Lost Gospel: The Book of Q and Christian Origins* (San Francisco: HarperSanFrancisco, 1993).

13. See Robert W. Funk and Roy W. Hoover et al., *The Five Gospels: The Search for the Authentic Words of Jesus* (New York: Macmillan, 1993).

14. See E. P. Sanders, *Jesus and Judaism* (Philadelphia: Fortress Press, 1985).

15. See Jon Sobrino, *Jesus the Liberator* (Maryknoll, N.Y.: Orbis Books, 1993).

16. See N. T. Wright, *Jesus and the Victory of God* (Minneapolis: Fortress Press, 1996).

17. See Paul Winter, *On the Trial of Jesus* (Berlin: Walter de Gruyter, 1961).

18. Raymond E. Brown, *The Death of the Messiah: From Gethsemane to the Grave: A Commentary on the Passion Narratives in the Four Gospels* (New York: Doubleday, 1994), 4.

19. John Dominic Crossan, *Who Killed Jesus? Exposing the Roots of Anti-Semitism in the Gospel Story of the Death of Jesus* (San Francisco: HarperSanFrancisco, 1995), 8.

20. See Jacob Neusner, *Judaism: The Evidence of the Mishnah*, 2d ed. (Atlanta: Scholars Press, 1988).

21. J. Andrew Overman, *Matthew's Gospel and Formative Judaism* (Minneapolis: Fortress Press, 1990), 160.

22. Anthony J. Saldarini, *Matthew's Christian-Jewish Community* (Chicago: University of Chicago Press, 1994), 198.

# 4. HISTORICAL JESUS RESEARCH
## Its Relevance to Thoughtful Christians and to Systematic Theologians

*Monika K. Hellwig*

Ever since the scientific quest for the historical Jesus was launched by Lutheran scholars in German universities in the nineteenth century, thoughtful Christians have been challenged and troubled by it. Thoughtless Christians, of course, were neither challenged nor troubled because they simply rejected whatever they learned from such research, condemning it as an impious attack on the faith that need not be taken seriously. Unfortunately, this attitude has not been confined to the ignorant among Christian believers. It has often included church leaders who have done their best to keep information about the quest for the historical Jesus away from church members, presumably to shelter them from temptations against the faith.

With the advance of the media age, nothing is secret, and nothing can be kept safely hidden in scholarly circles and esoteric publications. In this context, the continuing research in quest of the historical Jesus concerns all of us. Every thoughtful Christian is challenged to evaluate the disparate messages that come from scholars in the field, and we systematic theologians cannot escape the task of making our own evaluations. We need to assess first the trustworthiness of the claims of the specialist scholars publishing on the topic, then the relevance of the research for the way we have been doing systematic Christology, and finally how to reformulate our systematic Christology to be intelligible to the contemporary believer and consistent with the research findings, but also in continuity with the traditions of the faith.

Luke Timothy Johnson's essay in this volume offers a specialist's critique of recent turns Jesus research has taken. Daniel Harrington's deals in some detail with one area of Jesus research that has been especially fruitful for Christian faith and for systematic understanding of Jesus and his role, namely, the Jewishness of Jesus with all that it implies. The scope of this essay will be threefold: to consider the sources of our Christology and the role that the word of scripture plays among them in the Catholic tradition; to report briefly on developments in Christology in the twentieth century, especially as they have impinged on Catholic faith and practice; and to reflect on what this means for the Christian believer, especially in a Catholic context.

## The Sources of Christology

The implications of Jesus research for Catholic theologians and believers are different from the impact such research can have on those Christians who profess a faith defined by scripture alone. In the Catholic context, the scriptures are the book of the church, the collection of documents that arose out of the existing tradition of the faithful and that crystallized some but not all of the testimonies, convictions, and reflections of the community of the faithful. These texts were edited, selected, and gathered to be normative for the future, but not to hold exclusive authority. The living experience and testimony of the church, the cumulative wisdom arising out of lives of discipleship and prayerful reflection on the experience of discipleship, are interwoven with the written words of scripture, elucidating the meaning of text in ever unfolding ways. In this process, there is a certain dialectic with the scholarly function that clarifies the meaning of text in a different way—from research that fills in the context, clarifies the meaning of vocabulary, studies literary genre, and so forth. There is certainly a significant role for both kinds of interpretation of text, though on both sides there are those who would make their own type of interpretation exclusive.[1]

When Christians reflect on the person, mission, and significance of Jesus of Nazareth in our time, they have a long history of discipleship, reflection, and interpretation behind them, some of which has taken on a normative character shaping future reflection. The earliest Christians, of course, had the living memory of those who had known Jesus in the flesh as well as the experience of new life and power exploding in the

community of the risen Jesus. They had no need of scholarship to eluci-
date the context of the teaching and life and death, because they were
still living in the same context and took it for granted as the background to the narratives they repeated, the exhortations they remembered, and the interpretations they put upon the events. While they
remained a community in the Hebrew context, they had no need of
specialized scholarship to unfold the Hebrew scriptures, because this
was going on around them all the time and had shaped their own lives
and thinking.

A second phase in Christology began when, in the increasing communities of Gentile converts, interpretation in Hebrew terms became
less familiar and intelligible, and questions in terms of the Greek
thought-world became more urgent. With this shift there came the
ontological preoccupation that took the center of the stage for many
centuries. The questions about the person, mission, and significance of
Jesus centered not on "who is Jesus?" but rather "what is Jesus?" Of what
nature—human, divine, or demigod? The councils of the fourth, fifth,
and subsequent centuries left a strange legacy. Quite against the
declared intention of most of them, notably the much cited Council of
Chalcedon, the assertion of the true divinity of Jesus so obscured his
full and authentic humanity that the historical context and events of his
life came to seem irrelevant. His humanity continued to be asserted in
the standard Christology, but as though it were a timeless, uncontextu-
alized humanity, fixed in history almost accidentally by insistence on
his birth from the Virgin Mary and his death by crucifixion under
Pontius Pilate, leaving the intervening life as though it had little importance.[2] The birth was by divine intervention and the death by the will
of the Father, reducing his humanity for many of the faithful to his ability to suffer physical pain. Throughout the medieval period in the West,
the faithful grasped at this as at a straw, building their devotions around
the physical pain of Jesus and around the ampler human experience of
Mary the mother of Jesus.

A third phase in Christology began in the nineteenth century with
two parallel movements: the German scientific quest for the historical
Jesus, tending to minimize his meaning for faith and theology; and the

English (and later French and German) Catholic tradition of composing "lives of Christ," exercises of the informed imagination that tried to picture what it would have been like to be with him in his preaching journeys through Galilee, Samaria, and Judea, and what he himself felt and thought. These latter bold attempts to take the humanity of Jesus seriously were in part the work of Jesuits, no doubt arising out of the Ignatian heritage of the *Spiritual Exercises*, which in turn developed from medieval texts of piety. Such "lives," used as spiritual reading and as a basis for spiritual retreats, certainly roused an appetite to know more about the historical Jesus from a stance, not of skepticism, but of devotion.

When, therefore, a Catholic Christian in our time reflects on the person, mission, and significance of Jesus, the sources for such reflection will be many: the devotional practices that may have made the strongest impact, the sacramental life and activity of the church including its preaching, the catechisms memorized or studied in childhood, and the iconography that has made its unnoticed but strong impact. Many devout believers have developed a great capacity to compartmentalize the content of these sources of input so that intrinsically disturbing messages from contemporary scientific research are often bracketed as something to think about later, or something only to be understood by specialists, or something that makes sense to unbelievers but not to believers. However, the more thoughtful know that sooner or later they will have to deal with these disturbing messages for the sake of the integrity of their faith. And that presents an inescapable task to the systematic theologian.

When the Catholic theologian reflects on the person, mission, and significance of Jesus, the sources that come into play include: a well-established doctrinal position, developed mainly out of the definition of Chalcedon and the prior conciliar statements cited by that council; the biblical testimony, which for many centuries was not well integrated into the doctrinal tradition; personal insights and understanding derived from discipleship; and all kinds of often unrecognized assumptions based on liturgy, devotional customs, iconography, Christian fiction, and other currents of lived Catholicism in all its exuberant manifestations.[3]

For the Catholic theologian of the twentieth century, the task of taking biblical scholarship seriously, becoming thoroughly acquainted with it, and finding ways to integrate it coherently into a doctrinal tradition that grew to great complexity over many centuries using nonbiblical categories, is a formidable task.

## Developments in Twentieth-Century Christology

A number of strands have combined in the process of twentieth-century Catholic Christology to make it at once more hospitable and more critical towards biblical scholarship. A preoccupation early in the century with the consciousness of Jesus certainly suggested that not everything can be extrapolated from dogmatic assumptions and that the testimony preserved in the Gospels should play some role in this, even when it is granted that the Gospels are not, and were not intended to be, a simple, straightforward chronicle of events. It became clear that in order to take this testimony into account, theologians must concern themselves with the continuing research of scripture scholars rather more specifically than had been their custom.

Another strand in the process was the movement that began in France early in the century, prompting lay people both individually and in small action groups to read and meditate on the Gospels. Out of this movement arose demands for commentaries suitable for Catholic laity, taking account of the doctrinal positions of the church while elucidating the Gospel passages in such a way as to support orthodox styles of piety. The questions that arose out of such circles challenged customary teaching in Christology quite sharply, not so much on the basis of its truth claims but rather on its intelligibility. As more lay people became interested in studying theology as an aid to piety, those teaching theology commonly found that their own theological formation was inadequate to the task.

Out of this search for greater intelligibility came such promethean endeavors as those of Karl Rahner and Edward Schillebeeckx. Rahner's foundational contribution to theology generally was his critique of the epistemology of theological statements from an existentialist perspective: we can only come to understanding by beginning with the resources of our own subjectivity.[4] In Christology, his foundational contribution was the methodological principle of "ascending Christology," namely, the attempt to understand by beginning with what we know of being human and proceeding from there, as the earliest Christians certainly did, to an attempt to understand what is meant by the divinity claim for Jesus.[5] This can be stated otherwise as moving from the known to the unknown. For Rahner himself, throughout his long theological career, this remained at the existential level rather than the historical. Many of his former students, however, swiftly saw the historical implications that must draw both biblical text and biblical scholarship into the discussion. To be truly human is not only to be in some sense essentially human, but to be existentially, specifically, and concretely human. From this, J. B. Metz grappled with the political context of the life of Jesus and his actions and stances. Many Latin American scholars, notably Gustavo Gutierrez, Ignacio Ellacuria, and Jon Sobrino, grappled with the economic implications for understanding the mind and intentions of Jesus.

In all these cases it was clear that historical Jesus research was critical to the theological enterprise, though it became equally clear that historical Jesus researchers were by no means in agreement among themselves concerning the interpretation to be placed on their findings. In fact, diligent and well-meaning theologians who had gone to great lengths to acquaint themselves with contemporary scripture scholarship often found themselves under sharp attack from one scripture scholar or group for following the interpretations of another. Nowhere was this more acute than in the case of the Latin American liberation theologians, who found that not all prominent scripture scholars were alerted to the partiality of their own hermeneutic circles; many had come to their historical Jesus research with some very strong assumptions about the distinction between political and spiritual issues, and used their standing as scripture scholars to promote a privatizing concept of Christian faith and discipleship and (indirectly) a conservative political agenda.[6] Nevertheless, Third World liberation theologians are intensely aware that historical Jesus research is critical to their enterprise, and that they must continue to struggle to evaluate the disparate testimonies coming from New Testament scholars of various schools and persuasions.

An area in which the collaboration has gone far more happily is that of research into the Jewishness of Jesus. Champions for the importance of this study arose early in the century out of ecumenical efforts in Jewish-Christian relations. What began as scholarly courtesy and good-will toward Jews of our own time has in the course of this century greatly enriched and enlightened Christians concerning their own faith tradition. For systematic Christology, the research into the Hebrew context for the life, teaching, and actions of Jesus still holds immense possibilities for transcending the apparent gridlock on the way to contemporary intelligibility—a gridlock constituted by customary post-Chalcedonian interpretations of Chalcedon. While Chalcedon insists that the one person Jesus is fully and truly human, although we truthfully claim divinity for him, subsequent repetition rearranged the formula to assert that the one divine person is also human but not a human person, thereby turning both the intention and the wording of Chalcedon upside down. The recovery of Hebrew traditions promises a breakthrough in categories for retracing our historical steps and retrieving meaning.[7]

All these strands have come together in the magisterial synthesis offered by Edward Schillebeeckx in his great trilogy.[8] In addition to his gathering of so much scripture scholarship into the foundation for his systematic reflection, Schillebeeckx makes a critical point about the very definition of historical Jesus scholarship.[9] To know any historical person, he points out, is largely a matter of knowing the impact that that person has had on the lives and thinking of others and on subsequent history. In that sense we know a great deal about the person of Jesus who has left a long-term, far-flung, complex, and ever unfolding legacy. The records we have in the Gospels are scanty and stylized, but they are a trustworthy testimony precisely because they come from the community of disciples. Contemporary non-Christian witnesses are even scantier, but they give certain kinds of information reliably. Contextual study is useful for interpreting direct testimony, especially where it illumines otherwise obscure sayings or references. But all of these together are not the full testimony; they are elements of a story that is much greater than any of the elements and that includes in the history of the disciples the great and enduring impact Jesus has had and continues to have in the world.

The conclusion, then, is that in our time, as in the nineteenth century, minimizing assessments of what we know of Jesus, and therefore of his significance, based on a narrow construction of what is truth and how we know truth, what is history and how we know history, miss the larger reality that is the object of faith, not because that object is obscure, hypothetical, or undocumented, but because it is too large to see with certain lenses.

## What Does It Mean for the Believer?

The ordinary, that is nonspecialist, believer is too easily subjected to bombardment by sensational media reports. Because Jesus research has become highly technical and specialized, most people are not able to discriminate and evaluate. It is important that they be alerted through preaching, adult education, popularly written books, lectures, discussions, and colloquia such as those that formed the basis for this book, of the proper role of such scholarship and the limits of what it can provide.

In principle, research about the historical Jesus is a support to faith because it helps understanding. The stance that rejects all critical study as impious is not helpful because it is a refusal to be open to truth, a prejudice, a judgment before the evidence has been presented. Uncritical acceptance of whatever appears in the more sensational press is also not helpful. What can the nonspecialist do? The believer can read and listen with the awareness that a faith tradition that has shaped the lives, hopes, and good deeds of many people for many centuries will not suddenly be invalidated by the controverted findings of a particular group of contemporary scholars, though it may gain further depth and solidity. Further, the believer can become more conversant with the faith tradition, read what believing scripture scholars have to say about the more sensational findings, continue to study and reflect prayerfully, and seek out theologians who can integrate new findings into traditional Christology.

Not all Jesus research currently being done and published is shocking or confusing to the believer. Some is simply enlightening and therefore helpful, and this includes not only research by Christian scholars, but a great deal of the research by Jewish scholars, some of which is discussed in the subsequent essays of this volume.

NOTES

1. For the latest official church statement on the way the role of scripture within the tradition is regarded in Catholic perspective, see *Catechism of the Catholic Church* (London: Chapman, 1994), 23–35.

2. Cf. the classic creeds, such as the Apostles' Creed and the Nicene (Nicaeno-Constantinopolitan) Creed, both dating in their present form from the fourth century. The shaping of the formal definitions of the fourth- and fifth-century councils is set out very thoroughly in chronological order by Alois Grillmeier in *Christ and Christian Tradition: From the Apostolic Age to Chalcedon*, trans. J. S. Bowden (New York: Sheed & Ward, 1965).

3. A summary of the present customary synthesis of Christology in the Catholic tradition, which has the official hierarchic sanction of the church, is to be found in *Catechism of the Catholic Church*, 96–158.

4. Rahner's own account of this contribution is available in *Foundations of Christianity*, trans. William V. Dych (New York: Seabury Press, 1978), 24–89.

5. Ibid., 178–292.

6. An excellent account of this development and the arguments involved is given by Arthur F. McGovern, *Liberation Theology and Its Critics* (Maryknoll, N.Y.: Orbis Books, 1989), 62–82.

7. For some indications of possible directions for future development, see *Jews and Christians Speak of Jesus*, ed. Arthur E. Zannoni (Minneapolis: Fortress Press, 1994), 125–50.

8. Edward Schillebeeckx, *Jesus: An Experiment in Christology*, trans. Hubert Hoskins (New York: Seabury Press, 1979); Edward Schillebeeckx, *Christ: The Experience of Jesus as Lord*, trans. John Bowden (New York: Crossroad, 1981); Edward Schillebeeckx, *Church: The Human Story of God*, trans. John Bowden (New York: Crossroad, 1991).

9. See Schillebeeckx, *Jesus*, 41–102.

# 5. JEWISH REFLECTIONS ON JESUS
## Some Abiding Trends
*Michael J. Cook*

Serious Jewish study of Jesus emerged during the 1800s in Europe. For centuries, Jewish life there had remained stagnant behind ghetto walls while society was undergoing remarkable change due to the discovery of the New World, the Renaissance, the Protestant Reformation, and the commercial and industrial revolutions. When the ghetto walls were flung open, however, largely as a result of Napoleon's conquest of Europe, Jews were forced to come to terms with Christianity and, in so doing, to put aside centuries of Jewish misconceptions about Jesus. They were aided by a new development in the Christian sector termed, in retrospect, the "old quest for the historical Jesus." Christian scholars, wishing to reconstruct Jesus' life against his specifically Jewish context, discerned the possible relevance of ancient rabbinic writings in fleshing out this milieu. Eventually, Jewish scholars were invited to help explain the nuances of these Hebrew and Aramaic texts.

Jewish historians began to include in their works chapters on Christian origins in relation to the Jewish context of Jesus' time. This modern Jewish research contrasted sharply with previous Jewish attitudes in three respects:

(1) In ancient and medieval times, Jewish tradition had caricatured Jesus as a sorcerer who attempted to beguile the Jewish people and lead them astray.[1] Modern Jewish scholarship, by contrast, restored respectability to his image, even reclaiming Jesus as a Jew who established no new religion! Elements of Christianity that produced its break from Judaism were now assigned to timeframes after Jesus' death.

(2) With Jesus now revealed as fully loyal to Judaism, Jews had to reconsider why their forebears had been so precipitous in favoring his

95

execution. Modern Jewish "rehabilitation" of Jesus now required reevaluation of reasons for his arrest, eventuating in the judgment that Roman officialdom, not Jewish authorities, must have played the determinative role in his death. The Evangelists' fear of Rome had conditioned their portrait of Pilate's attempted exoneration of Jesus a generation or two earlier, and had prompted them to shift responsibility for Jesus' condemnation from Roman onto Jewish elements instead.

(3) While in earlier centuries Jews had routinely traced the separation between Judaism and Christianity to alleged apostasy by Jesus, modern Jews now switched that decisive role to Paul.

Does Jewish scholarship today remain consistent with these revised contours? Much depends upon how we define Jewish scholarship. Some Jewish scholars identify themselves as such on theological grounds, others on ethnic or cultural bases. For some, Jewish self-identification has no bearing on their scholarship; for others, it has a significant bearing. In addition to the normal diversity among scholars in general, we also commonly hear the expression, "two Jews, three opinions."

Respecting one of the overarching themes of this volume—Jesus and Christian origins through Jewish eyes—I will be culling from my experiences in teaching rabbinical students, rabbis, and well-read Jewish laypersons to ask whether, and if so how, Jewish affiliation and orientation may condition views Jews commonly hold of Jesus. I have found the following orientations to be characteristic of most Jewish readers:

- a detachment of sorts, for the New Testament is not scripture for the Jew;

- a disproportionate tendency for many Jewish readers of the New Testament to become preoccupied with those sections, motifs, or narrative episodes that seem to impinge upon Jews and Judaism; and

- a sadness, for these Jews will likely view the anti-Jewish tendencies within the New Testament, particularly the Gospels, against the backdrop of a later regrettable history in whose development the New Testament was so decisively influential.

The modern Jewish disposition to reclaim Jesus as a Jew has also spurred many Jewish readers:

- to posit and then to identify late accretions allegedly superimposed upon the historical Jesus by the developing Church—the expectation being that, to the degree such accretions can now be successfully stripped away, a more thoroughly Jewish Jesus will be discovered; and

- to question Jesus' commonly presumed distance from Pharisaism by relying, instead, on studies of seeming parallels between Jesus' teachings and those found in the later rabbinic literature.

From such readership, I have distilled what I believe to be five characteristically Jewish approaches to processing Gospel presentations of Jesus.[2]

*PERSPECTIVE 1: Changes in Christianity's self-perception vis-à-vis Judaism occasioned corresponding adjustments in portrayals of Jesus' stance toward Jews and Judaism as presented in the Gospels.*

Almost universally, Jewish readers will discover what they deem to be inconsistencies in Jesus' behavior toward fellow Jews. Sometimes he urges love of peace and turning the other cheek; elsewhere, however, he appears vindictive and vitriolic toward many in the Jewish community. How may Jews reconcile the Jesus who insists that "every one who is [even] angry with his brother shall be liable to judgment" (Matt 5:22) with the Jesus who decries the Pharisees as "you serpents, you brood of vipers, how are you to escape being sentenced to hell?" (Matt 23:33); or the Jesus who instructs listeners to "love your enemies . . . pray for those who persecute you" (Matt 5:44), with one castigating Jews "who had believed in him" as being "of your father the devil . . . a murderer from the beginning . . ., a liar and the father of lies" (John 8:31, 44)?

Inevitably, many Jewish readers will infer that such conflicting images of Jesus must be viewed developmentally. Thus,

- during a pre-Pauline phase, emergent Christianity, perceiving itself still within Judaism, naturally preserved or generated portrayals of Jesus as faithful to Judaism;

- later, when Christianity became more conscious of its own individuality and regretful that Jews continued to avoid the Church, Jesus' figure was adjusted to reflect regret at Jewish opaqueness to Christian truths;

- later still, as interchange between Christians and Jewish opponents became increasingly contentious, regret became supplanted by hostility toward Jews, with Jesus' figure enlisted to support this accrued bitterness: Jesus himself now became portrayed as hostile toward Jews.

What intimations of Jesus' consonance with Judaism do Jewish readers posit for the first phase? Most often, the Great Commandment (Mark 12:28–34a),[3] the Lord's Prayer (Matt 6:9–13),[4] and parables of the kingdom.[5] Reflecting the second phase would be echoes of Romans 9–11. The third period manifests hostility through words ascribed to Jesus (e.g., "woes" against the Pharisees [Matthew 23] and passages in John that seem abrasive [5:42, 45–46; 6:53; 8:23–24, 37–38, 44–47] or seem to present Jesus outside the fold of the Jewish people [10:34; 13:33]) and through channels other than Jesus' words (e.g., the Sanhedrin trial [Mark 14:53ff. and parallels] and the Barabbas episode [Mark 15:6ff. and parallels] with its infamous "blood curse" [Matt 27:24–25], together with editorial characterizations impugning the Jews' motives and maligning their conduct).

I personally find this approach problematic for the following reasons:

- Nothing precludes Jesus himself from having espoused all three positions (fidelity, regret, and hostility).

- New Testament scholars have achieved no consensus in distinguishing statements authentic to Jesus from those formed by the later Church, so compartmentalization of various Jesus images by Jews can seem arbitrary.

- Jewish readers loosely apply form-critical methods that conveniently result in the very kind of Jesus they desire. The more they strip away Gospel traditions attributable to the later Gentile

Church the more characteristically Jewish the Jesus who remains turns out to be.

- Recourse by Jewish readers to rabbinic literature—in order to discover presumed parallels to Jesus' teachings (and to establish thereby his proximity to Pharisaism)—is often methodologically flawed.[6]

- It is arduous to explain why Christianity ever traced its origins to a Jesus who presumably departed in no significant way from the diversified Judaism(s) of his own day.

These ostensibly formidable objections to this approach may still not disable it, because the core assertion remains compelling: Since the developing self-perception of some Christian elements vis-à-vis Judaism most likely did express itself in consecutive phases of consonance, then regret, ultimately supplanted by hostility, some corresponding adjustments in Jesus' image would inevitably have been forthcoming. Problems in exegeting particular passages do not then necessarily undermine the hypothesis in general, since what breaks down is not the hypothesis itself as much as specific attempts to prove it. Respecting phase one, that Jesus' immediate followers remained within the synagogue and continued to abide by Jewish practice, argues that they identified Jesus himself as having been consonant with Jewish belief and practice. Respecting the end of the process (phase three), the intensity of Gospel denunciations of Jews can still most plausibly be assigned to well after Jesus' death, when Christianity's attitude toward many Jews had become suffused with hostility.[7]

*PERSPECTIVE 2: The various ways in which Paul's theology was understood influenced the Gospel portraits of Jesus.*

Since Paul's epistles are our earliest Christian writings, Paul's thinking may have influenced directions of differing segments of Christianity—both those adhering to Pauline views and those resistant to Paul but forced, nonetheless, to address his thinking. To be emphasized is not what Paul said or intended but rather the influential role those interpreting Paul—even in widely diverging fashions—played in how Jesus later came to be portrayed in Gospel traditions.

The conceptualization here by many Jewish readers is that the earliest images of the historical Jesus and his teachings were filtered through Paul's interpretation of the meaning of the Christ, the consequence being that Jesus' image and teachings were not simply preserved but also embellished, in some cases significantly transformed. Respecting subsequent Christian-Jewish relations, three themes of decisive importance were generated through this process, each bearing the impress either of what Paul himself preached, or of how others construed, or misconstrued, that preaching:

- the motif of rejection of the Law of Moses;

- the motif of Christian missionaries turning the focus of their preaching away from Jews and toward Gentiles instead; and

- the motif of Jews as superseded by Gentiles as God's chosen people.

While some Gospel traditions depict Jesus himself espousing these motifs, many Jewish readers suspect that Jesus never actually broke with the Law, or counseled a turning away from Jews and toward Gentiles instead, or sanctioned notions of the Jews as superseded by Gentiles.[8] Since these three themes contributed centrally to the stereotyping of Jesus as an apostate by ancient and medieval Jewish tradition, as well as to supersessionist and triumphalist theology of some Christians past and present, suggestions that these motifs derive more from how Paul was interpreted than from what Jesus personally espoused would carry significant ramifications!

Is this second approach problematic? Yes, in these respects:

- It analyzes Paul only on the basis of his epistles. What about the book of Acts, which presents a decidedly more rabbinic Paul, trained by Gamaliel (22:3), often supportive of the Law (16:3; 18:18; 21:20ff.; 25:8; 26:4ff.), and ostensibly more involved in missionizing directly to Jews as well as to Gentiles?

- How do we know whether Paul's writings were even known by the Gospel writers?

- Is it not problematic ascribing to Paul every Christian departure from Judaism, as if Paul founded a Christianity having no threads of connectedness with Jesus?

- Why not argue that Paul's teachings were consonant with those of Jesus? For example, that Paul did not originate the idea of a mission to Gentiles but only extrapolated a latency within Jesus, who expected an imminent end to the world order—and within the parameters of Jewish scriptural anticipation of Gentile involvement in that new era?[9]

Telltale clues may yet buttress this Jewish approach.[10] Why was there the violent opposition to Paul from pillars of the Jerusalem church when he ate with Gentiles, presumably breaking Jewish dietary laws, and began bringing Gentiles directly into the Christian fold (cf. Gal 1:18–2:21)? Why did not James, Cephas, and John recognize Paul's consonance with Jesus, if, as some Gospel texts attest, Jesus himself had departed from the Law (cf. especially Mark 7:19) and had counseled or predicted a turning to Gentiles?[11] Would this not suggest that Jesus himself had never broken with the Law or counseled a turning from his own people to Gentiles?[12]

Second, if Jesus had indeed "declared all foods clean" (Mark 7:19), why did Peter (in Acts 10:14) not know this or need a thrice-stated revelation (v. 16) concerning what he should have remembered from Jesus personally? Would this not suggest that Jesus himself had never nullified dietary laws?

Third, if Jesus had publicly transgressed the Sabbath or justified transgression by his disciples (as, e.g., in Mark 2:23–3:5), how could Paul's Judaizing opponents in Galatia have insisted on Jewish calendrical observance (Gal 4:9–11) or on general adherence to the same Law Jesus himself had presumably disavowed? Would not this suggest that Jesus himself had never broken with the Law, let alone counseled departures therefrom by others?

Fourth, why, when Paul argued the issue of the Law, did he not draw for support upon Jesus' teachings (resembling those recorded, later, in the Gospels)? Instead, he argued only on general grounds that faith in Christ constitutes the sole way to salvation. Such recourse to specific teachings of Jesus would have been not only useful but also vitally persuasive to others, especially since food and Sabbath issues were sorely troubling problems for Paul (Gal 2:11–14; 4:10; Rom 14:1–6, 13–23). Would not Paul's failure to take advantage of those teachings by Jesus imply that Jesus had not originally been known to have advanced such teachings to start with?

These problems suggest to many Jewish readers that Pauline thought, after Jesus' ministry, first stimulated the raising of these issues, and that Jesus' intimate followers vigorously opposed Paul—perceiving him as distancing himself from what they remembered as Jesus' fidelity to the Law and to the Jewish people.

Objections to Perspective 2, meanwhile, are themselves open to challenge: (1) Reliance on Acts may well misrepresent Paul.[13] (2) Gospel writers may very well have known of Paul and been aware of his epistles.[14] (3) Paul's capacity to reinterpret Jesus' significance along lines divergent from earliest understandings (witness his elaborations concerning crucifixion and resurrection) prompts insistence that, with Paul, Christianity experienced renewal, redirection, even radical transformation. (4) As for issues of latency, should Gal 2:15 mean that Jews, also, in order to be saved, must actually forgo the Law, this would exceed mere latency from Jesus! When Paul reverses the sequence for salvation, so that now "the full number of Gentiles" will precede disbelieving Israel (Rom 11:25–26), this would exceed any latency within Jesus toward Gentiles. Also distinctive is Paul's argument on supersession: that the covenant skipped from Abraham to Christ, with membership now restricted to those in Christ irrespective of whether they are Israel biologically (Rom 9:6ff.).

Thus, Perspective 2 may remain compelling to many Jewish readers who cannot otherwise unravel why a Jewish messianic claimant would diverge from the Law, or counsel a turning from Jews to Gentiles, or redefine chosenness in terms of Gentiles superseding Jews. Paul's significant variance from Judaism precisely on these issues convinces many Jews that his influence came to transform Jesus' image into what we now find it to be in many Gospel formulations.

*PERSPECTIVE 3: In the process of responding to challenges by Jewish opponents, emerging Christianity adjusted or added to Jesus-traditions teachings and nuances not authentic to Jesus' ministry; accordingly, teachings ascribed to Jesus—and impinging on Jews and Judaism—should not be viewed only as an undifferentiated mass.*

Between Jesus' ministry (circa 30 C.E.) and the completion of the Gospels (70–100 C.E.), dilemmas arose for emerging churches. Some of these problems stemmed from challenges that non-Christian Jews directed against Jesus' credentials and against the validity of Christian preaching about him. Despite the Gospels' ostensible preoccupation with retelling details of Jesus' ministry decades earlier, these texts were also addressing more recently surfacing concerns—issues so formidable that Christianity had to enlist Jesus' authoritative image to solve them. Conceiving that their own immediate problems had already originated during Jesus' day, and that solutions were therefore discoverable in his words and deeds, the Evangelists often recast his actual teachings to render them germane for later circumstances, as the following illustrations attest:

(1) Noting that some Christians failed to abide by Jewish dietary laws, Jews posed a challenge to Christian opponents: How can you profess to fulfill God's covenant while violating the laws of *kashrut*? In helping his constituents to respond, Mark (7:18–23) adjusted a genuine teaching of Jesus to mean something other than what was originally intended—redirecting Jesus' words, "Do you not see that whatever goes into a man from outside cannot defile him?" to mean that Jesus had "thus declared all foods clean" (7:19b). While Jesus' intent may have been to teach that what truly matters is internal moral consciousness, Mark instead applied Jesus' words to the different problem of dietary laws, so as to address a challenge from Jews, a challenge that first arose between the time of Jesus' ministry and the completion of Mark's Gospel forty years later.

(2) Christians asserting Jesus' messianic credentials were challenged by Jews who argued that Elijah, the Messiah's herald, had yet to appear—a test recorded in Mark 9:11: "Why do the scribes say that first

Elijah must come?" Ultimately, Christian tradition conformed John the Baptist to Elijah's image, as in Mark 9:13 ("I tell you that Elijah has [already] come"), sharpened by Matt 17:13 ("Then the disciples understood that he was speaking to them of John the Baptist"). Additionally, John's death became attributed to an evil king and queen, Herod Antipas and Herodias, conforming this duo's role as well to that of their wicked counterparts, Ahab and Jezebel, who had sought Elijah's life.[15]

(3) Confronted by Jewish denials of the resurrection, Christianity came to advance an empty tomb tradition (unmentioned and, possibly, unknown by Paul[16]). Responding to this unexpected claim, Jewish skeptics ascribed the alleged emptiness of the tomb to the disciples' theft of the body, a charge Matthew tried to neutralize by his own proofs that a theft was manifestly impossible (cf. 27:62–66; 28:11–15). Suggestion of a theft was an inevitable Jewish retort to the empty tomb story. That Mark does not mention let alone cope with this response hints that the empty tomb tradition first surfaced either with Mark himself (who failed to anticipate the Jewish reaction) or only shortly before him (so insinuation of a "theft" had yet to surface to his attention)—revealing the tomb tradition as a Christian response to a Jewish challenge arising between Jesus' ministry and Mark's writing decades later.

PERSPECTIVE 4: *Study of the Gospels of Mark, Matthew, and Luke in parallel columns reveals that later writers intensified the anti-Judaism of their sources. Therefore, one might plausibly argue that anti-Judaism decreases as we regress toward Christian origins.*

Most New Testament scholarship holds that Matthew and Luke are not only literarily dependent upon Mark but have also altered his text. Accordingly, some variations from Mark may reflect intentional adjustments, not simply dependence on other sources. Plausibly, anti-Jewish nuances present in Matthew and Luke, yet absent from parallel material in Mark, could reflect the later editors' own inclinations, conditioned by tensions of Christian-Jewish discourse in their day. The following illustrations are apt:

*Jesus before the Sanhedrin (Mark 14:55–56; Matt 26:59–60).* Here the Matthean account significantly changes Mark's rendition by adding a single word: "false." While in Mark the Jewish officials sought what they apparently believed to be true testimony against Jesus, in Matthew they set about finding false testimony *ab initio*. In Mark's understanding, therefore, the Jewish authorities, genuinely believing Jesus guilty, had only to seek out honest witnesses to confirm their belief. Yet Matthew implies that because Jewish authorities knew Jesus to be innocent, they actually had to seek out specifically false witnesses to condemn him! Thus, does a Matthean adjustment of Mark heighten an already earlier anti-Jewish tendency of the Christian tradition.[17]

*The question concerning tribute to Caesar (Mark 12:13–17; Matt 22:15–22).* Here Mark deems Jesus' Jewish opponents hypocritical (v. 15), but Matthew decries them as malicious as well (v. 18). Thus, while both accounts are virtually identical, Matthew paints the Jewish leaders a shade more callous. He also has them disparaged by Jesus' own words rather than solely by the detached judgment of the narrator.

*The Great Commandment (Mark 12:28–34; Matt 22:34–40).* Here is the single Markan instance of camaraderie between Jesus and a Jewish leader! But the pleasant conversation in Mark is transformed by Matthew into a confrontation where, from the very start, the Jewish leader's intent is not to engage Jesus amicably but rather "to test him" (v. 35). Moreover, not only is Mark's exchange of mutual admiration between Jesus and the Jewish scribe (12:32–34) edited out by Matthew, but so also the most important sentence of Jesus' Great Commandment: "Hear, O Israel: the Lord our God, the Lord is one" (cf. Mark 12:29). Quite evidently, Matthew does not wish to preserve this notice of friendly relations between Jesus and a Jewish leader; he also alters Jesus' Great Commandment so that it is no longer directed preeminently to the Jewish people!

*The Sentence of Death (Mark 15:12–15; Matt 27:22–26; Luke 23:21–25).* In Mark, the Roman governor, Pontius Pilate, attempts to acquit Jesus (v. 14), and it is the Jewish mob who calls for Jesus' crucifixion. Matthew's incorporation of the so-called blood curse (vv. 24–25), however, intensifies the Jews' culpability even as it further downplays Pilate's own involvement. Luke, by emphatically employing the third person, likewise heightens the Jews' accountability: "they were urgent, demanding with loud cries that he should be crucified"; "and their voices prevailed" (v. 23); "that their demand should be granted" (v. 24); "the man . . . whom they asked for"; "delivered up to their will" (v. 25). Luke also has Pilate acquit Jesus three times (23:4, 14, 22) rather than merely once (cf. Mark 15:14; Matt 27:23).

Just as Matthew and Luke revised their sources, Mark edited his own received traditions, transforming into confrontation teachings of Jesus not originally uttered in contexts of controversy.[18] Such observations are compatible with Perspective 1. The further we recede into earliest Christianity—approaching the time frame of Jesus himself—the more plausibly may Gospel expressions of anti-Judaism be understood as stemming from the developing church rather than from Jesus' ministry.

PERSPECTIVE 5: *A major reason why passages in the Jewish Bible seem to predict the coming of Jesus is that the Christian tradition came to model Jesus' image in conformity with Jewish scriptural imagery.*

For centuries, missionaries have drummed home to Jews a steady staccato of proof texts from Jewish scripture, citations said to prove that Jesus, and Jesus alone, fulfilled predictions of the Messiah's coming. See, for example, the apparent correspondence of Jesus with Isaiah's "Suffering Servant" (42:1–4; 49:1–6; 50:4–9; 52:13–53:12); or of Jesus' entry to Jerusalem on a donkey with its presumed prediction by Zechariah (9:9); or of the scene and words of Jesus on the cross with imagery from Psalms (e.g., 22:1, 6–8, 16–18; 69:21). Such claims were likely stimulated by Paul's insistence that "Christ died . . . in accordance with the scriptures" and "was raised . . . in accordance with the scriptures" (1 Cor 15:3–4), reasoning rendering it likely that early Christians would look to Jewish scripture (at the time, their only scripture) to sustain their theological beliefs.

Reflective Jews have reasoned out a dynamic underpinning at least some of these ostensible correlations—namely, that developing Gospel tradition fashioned details of Jesus' life to match predictions alleged to foretell him. The Evangelists did not possess data sufficient to flesh out accounts of Jesus' ministry. Once eyewitnesses of Jesus' ministry began to die off, the Jewish Bible became of potentially inestimable assistance!

Because Christians believed not only that Jesus was the Christ but also that scripture had predicted the Messiah's coming, they could readily see the Bible as prophesying Jesus in particular. If sufficient details about Jesus' ministry seemed unavailable, scripture could be combed as a ready repository of missing clues to which the image of Jesus could then be confidently conformed—since Jesus' ministry and Jewish scripture were presumed fully congruent one to the other.

Thus, the uncanny similarity of the Gospels' image of Jesus to Isaiah's "Suffering Servant" could have arisen from the specific likening of Jesus to the "Suffering Servant" model. Details of the scene on the cross (e.g., Jesus being scornfully mocked by passersby, with lots being cast for his garments) could fulfill Psalm 22 if they were enlisted therefrom! In Matthew, a misrendering of (the Hebrew) Zechariah's prediction (9:9) results in Jesus riding into Jerusalem on two animals simultaneously—a telltale indication of the lengths to which Gospel tradition could have gone in matching Jesus' image to its presumed scriptural anticipation.

An apt analogy would be to arrows shot at a blank wall, with bull's-eyes painted around them only thereafter! Reality, of course, would differ from appearance, for rather than arrows hitting targets, targets would have been accommodated to arrows. In some instances, at least, predictions from scripture would have served as arrows, with Jesus' image in the Gospels as the bull's-eye consciously—though in full faith and confidence—painted around each of them.[19]

To render this Jewish perspective more nuanced, it might be better to say that even regarding actual events in Jesus' life, scripture influenced which ones would be remembered. Thus, not only might narrators have created incidents "to give scriptural flavor" but from incidents that did occur narrators dramatized those capable of echoing the scriptures.[20] In either case, Jewish scripture played some significant formative role in the development of Jesus narratives.[21]

## Conclusion

In summary, since Jewish readers do not consider Jesus the Messiah or the New Testament their sacred scripture, their primary interests in reading the New Testament often lie with those passages impinging upon Jews and Judaism. Frequently, the theology of these texts seems curiously at variance with Judaism, sometimes even anti-Jewish as well. This is curious because the figures primarily advanced as espousing it, Jesus and Paul, were themselves Jews! Accordingly, many a Jewish reader has tended to process these materials in a manner rendering them less curious.

Thus, the seeming anomaly of a Pharisaic-like teacher of parables espousing a new "Christian" theology, at least implicitly anti-Jewish, is most acceptably resolved for some by reclaiming Jesus as a Jew and ascribing the Gospels' anti-Judaism instead to writers who had redirected the image of the historical Jesus along anti-Jewish lines. In surmising possible reasons for such alteration, many Jewish readers are drawn to the hostility that characterized Christian-Jewish relations in the Evangelists' own day, and also to the possible influence of Paul's theology on the Gospels' portrait of Jesus (whether or not Paul's theology was correctly understood and whether or not that understanding of Paul was being supported or opposed by the Evangelist in question). Jesus himself is thus spared responsibility for the Gospels' anti-Judaism, though the possibility that he had disputes with fellows Jews on particular issues is not thereby precluded. Later Christianity, in its issues with Jews—over challenges posed to the sufficiency of Jesus' messianic credentials and to the validity of the Christian message—readily enlisted Jesus' image for support, even though these were challenges concerning which he may have had neither any involvement nor even any antecedent awareness.

## NOTES

1. See Robert T. Herford, *Christianity in Talmud and Midrash* (London: Williams & Norgate, 1903); Joseph Klausner, *Jesus of Nazareth*, trans. Herbert Danby (New York: Macmillan, 1943), 17–54; Morris Goldstein, *Jesus in the Jewish Tradition* (New York: Macmillan, 1950); Jacob Z. Lauterbach, "Jesus in the Talmud," *Rabbinic Essays* (Cincinnati: Hebrew Union College Press, 1951), 471–570; David Catchpole, *The Trial of Jesus: A Study in the Gospels and Jewish Historiography from 1770 to the Present Day* (Leiden: E.J. Brill, 1971), 1–71.

2. Formulation of these five perspectives is my own. While of course not necessarily held by every Jewish reader, each perspective is nonetheless a predominant tendency. Early surveys of Jewish scholarship on Jesus and Christian origins yielding these types of conclusions include (alphabetically): Schalom Ben-Chorin, *Jesus im Judentum* (Wuppertal: Brockhaus, 1970); Schalom Ben-Chorim "The Image of Jesus in Modern Judaism," *Journal of Ecumenical Studies* 11 (summer 1974): 401–30; Herbert Danby, *The Jew and Christianity: Some Phases, Ancient and Modern, of the Jewish Attitude Towards Christianity* (London: Sheldon Press, 1927); Donald A. Hagner, *The Jewish Reclamation of Jesus: An Analysis and Critique of the Modern Jewish Study of Jesus* (Grand Rapids: Zondervan Publishing House, 1984); Walter Jacob, *Christianity through Jewish Eyes* (Cincinnati: Hebrew Union College, 1974); Jakob Jocz, *The Jewish People and Jesus Christ* (Grand Rapids: Baker Book House, 1979); Gösta Lindeskog, *Die Jesusfrage im Neuzeitlichen Judentum* (Darmstadt: Wissenschaftliche Buchgesellschaft, 1973); Claude G. Montefiore, "Jewish Conceptions of Christianity," *Hibbert Journal* 28 (January 1930): 246–60; Samuel Sandmel, *We Jews and Jesus* (New York: Oxford University Press, 1965); Thomas Walker, *Jewish Views of Jesus* (New York: Macmillan, 1931).

3. On the *Sh'ma*, cf. the liturgy of certain Jewish worship services, and Aqiba's last words at martyrdom (*Berakhoth* 61b); on loving one's neighbor, cf. the analogous teaching of Hillel (*Shabbat* 31a).

4. Cf. the *Qaddish* and Eighteen Benedictions. See Joseph Heinemann, "The Background of Jesus' Prayer in Jewish Liturgical Tradition," *The Lord's Prayer and Jewish Liturgy*, ed. Jakob J. Petuchowski and Michael Brocke (London: Burns & Oates, 1978) 81–99; Gordon J. Bahr, "The Use of the Lord's Prayer in the Primitive Church," *Journal of Biblical Literature* 84 (June 1965): 156ff.

5. The kingdom is a major theme in rabbinic literature and liturgy; cf. relevant sections of I. Abrahams, *Studies in Pharisaism and the Gospels* (repr. New York: KTAV Publishing House, 1967), and Claude G. Montefiore, *Rabbinic Literature and Gospel Teachings* (repr. New York: KTAV Publishing House, 1970). On the Parable of the Laborers in the Vineyard (Matt 20:1–16), cf. Jerusalem *Berakhoth* ii.3c; *Ecclesiastes Rabbah* 5:11; *Song of Songs Rabbah* 6:2; *Deuteronomy Rabbah* 6:1. On the Parable of the Marriage Feast (Matthew 22:1–14; Luke 14:16–24), see *Shabbat* 153a; cf. Jerusalem *Sanhedrin* vi.23c and *Lamentations Rabbah* 4:2. On the Parable of the Good Samaritan (Luke 15:11–32), see *Deuteronomy Rabbah* 2:24; cf. *Sotah* 9:15; *Sanhedrin* 38b. On the Parables of the Lost Coin (Luke 15:8–10) and the Hidden Treasure (Matt 13:44–46), cf. *Ecclesiastes Rabbah* 9:7 and *Song of Songs Rabbah* 1:1, 9. Care must be exercised in determining whether rabbinic parables that appear parallel to Gospel counterparts are genuinely so, and whether their context (date, place, function, etc.) makes such comparison meaningful.

6. See Michael J. Cook, "Jesus and the Pharisees," *Journal of Ecumenical Studies* 15 (summer 1978): 441–60 (especially p. 456); and Michael J. Cook, "Rabbinic Judaism and Early Christianity: From the Pharisees to the Rabbis," *Review and Expositor* 84 (spring 1987): 201–21.

7. Some scholars believe that the overwhelming percentage of Christians continued to perceive themselves within the Jewish people even into the 90s.
Accordingly, the tensions reported by the Gospels are essentially intra-Jewish disputes. Even on such a basis, hostility (in this case toward non-Christian Jews still
perceived as fellow Jews) would remain assignable to the post-70 time frame, and
Jesus' ostensibly hostile demeanor would remain a function of changes in
(Jewish) Christians' self-perception vis-à-vis non-Christian fellow Jews.

8. Cf. Hagner, *Jewish Reclamation of Jesus*, 87–132.

9. Consider that Isaiah, Micah, and Zechariah make allowance for inclusion of
Gentiles in the "end of days": "and many peoples shall . . . say: 'Come let us go up
to the mountain of the Lord . . . that we may walk in his paths'" (Isa 2:3.; cf. Mic
4:1ff.); "I will give you as a light to the nations" (Isa 49:6); "my justice [will be] for
a light to the peoples" (Isa 51:4); "thus says the Lord God, who gathers the out-
casts of Israel, 'I will gather yet others to him besides those already gathered'" (Isa
56:8; also 45:22; 66:19); "and many nations shall join themselves to the Lord in
that day" (Zech 2:11; also 8:20–23; cf. Tobit 14:6f.; Enoch 90:30–33).

10. E. P. Sanders frequently highlights the following kinds of anomaly (e.g., in
*Jesus and Judaism* [Philadelphia: Fortress Press, 1985]).

11. This problem was suggested early on by the Jewish historian Heinrich
Graetz in *Sinai et Golgotha, ou les origines du judaisme et du christianisme . . .* ,
trans. M. Hess (Paris: Michael Zevy Freres, 1867), 314–18, 392–407, 416–17; and
*History of the Jews* (Philadelphia: Jewish Publication Society of America, 1893)
2:155ff., 168–69; see also Paul Winter, *On the Trial of Jesus* (Berlin: Walter de
Gruyter, 1961), 113ff.; Samuel Sandmel, *The Genius of Paul* (Philadelphia:
Fortress Press, 1979), 38ff.

12. Matt 5:17ff. should not be brought into this discussion since it likely rep-
resents Matthew's reaction to Paul rather than any teaching by the historical
Jesus; see Michael J. Cook, "Interpreting 'Pro-Jewish' Passages in Matthew,"
*Hebrew Union College Annual* 54 (1983): 135–47.

13. See my discussion in "The Mission to the Jews in Acts: Unraveling Luke's
'Myth of the "Myriads,"'" in *Luke-Acts and the Jewish People: Eight Critical
Perspectives*, ed. J. Tyson (Minneapolis: Augsburg, 1988).

14. For example, Matthew's emphasis on Jesus as a lawgiver seems manifestly
a reaction to Pauline thought. As for Luke, see Morton S. Enslin, "'Luke' and
Paul," *Journal of the American Oriental Society* 58 (March 1938): 81–91; Morton
S. Enslin, "Once Again, Luke and Paul," *Zeitschrift für die Neutestamentliche
Wissenschaft und die Kunde der Alteren Kirche*, 61, nos. 3–4 (1970): 253–71. See
also John Knox: "I agree with Enslin that it is all but incredible that such a man
as Luke . . . should have been 'totally unaware that this hero of his had ever written
letters . . . Too many important churches owed their existence to [Paul] for his name
not to have been held in reverence in many areas and his work remembered. . . .'
Luke knew, or at least knew of, letters of Paul . . . and quite consciously and deliberately made little or no use of them" ("Acts and the Pauline Letter Corpus,"

*Studies in Luke-Acts*, ed. Leander E. Keck, Paul Schubert, and J. Louis Martyn [Philadelphia: Fortress Press, 1980], 283). Note how Paul himself quotes his opponents to the effect that "his letters are weighty and strong" (2 Cor 10:10)!

15. The artificiality of this Gospel solution becomes especially evident when we examine Josephus' *Antiquities* (18.116–19), which, describing John the Baptist without these Elijah trappings, conveys a far more credible account than do the Gospels of how, where, and why John died.

16. Paul repeats the tradition that Jesus "was buried" (1 Cor 15:4), but never says anything about a tomb (empty or otherwise).

17. Stated positively, Matthew's adjustment accentuates Jesus' innocence. Yet he accomplishes this by impugning the Jews' motives and behavior.

18. See Michael J. Cook, *Mark's Treatment of the Jewish Leaders* (Leiden: E. J. Brill, 1978).

19. Among Jewish scholars so reasoning, see Isaac Troki, *Faith Strengthened* (repr. New York: KTAV Publishing House, 1970); Gerard Sigal, *The Jew and the Christian Missionary: A Jewish Response to Missionary Christianity* (New York: KTAV Publishing House, 1981); David Berger and Michael Wyschogrod, *Jews and "Jewish Christianity"* (New York: KTAV Publishing House, 1978).

20. Raymond Brown, *The Death of the Messiah* (New York: Doubleday, 1994), 15: "The first followers of Jesus would have known . . . almost surely some of the details about Jesus' crucifixion, e.g., what kind of cross was employed. Nevertheless, what is preserved in the narrative is mostly what echoes Scripture (division of garments, offering of vinegary wine, final words of Jesus)."

21. See e.g., B. Lindars, *New Testament Apologetic* (London: SCM Press, 1961); J. Daniélou, *From Shadows to Reality: Studies in the Biblical Typology of the Fathers* (London: Burns & Oates, 1960); G. W. H. Lampe, "The Reasonableness of Typology," and K. J. Woollcombe, "The Biblical Origins and Patristic Development of Typology," *Essays on Typology* (Naperville, Ill.: Alec R. Allenson, 1957), 9–75; Robert H. Smith, "Exodus Typology in the Fourth Gospel," *Journal of Biblical Literature* 81 (December 1962): 329–42.

# 6. JESUS, DIVORCE, AND SEXUALITY
## A Jewish Critique[1]

*Amy-Jill Levine*

The American public's interest in what did, or did not, transpire between William Jefferson Clinton and Monica Lewinsky is symptomatic of a larger societal concern with morality and marital ethics. In 1997, the Promise Keepers rallied in Washington to pledge their lives to "traditional family values," while spokespeople from various women's advocacy groups condemned the gathering as a putsch for patriarchy. Covenant marriage is gaining increasing attention in state legislatures, as are initiatives to repeal sodomy laws and legalize same-sex relationships. The Roman Catholic practice of annulment was recently brought to public attention by a separation within the Kennedy family;[2] the plight of the *aguna* (the deserted wife) occasionally surfaces in the media,[3] as do instances of polygamy among groups who have separated from the main body of the Church of Jesus Christ of Latter-Day Saints. The Southern Baptist Convention's endorsement of the headship of the husband remains fodder for discussion and dissent, as does the current interest among some evangelicals in "courtship" as opposed to "dating."[4] While some Christian theologians insist that those who divorce and remarry, even in cases of spousal abuse, are committing sin, others see as sinful the clergy's frequent silence on domestic violence and counsel to the beaten wife that she should suffer "in Christ's name."

Pronouncements in the name of religion will always have a role in public morality and public policy. Too often, however, these voices are inflammatory or soporific rather than grounded and thoughtful. Too often scriptural passages are taken out of literary and cultural contexts; too often their complexities and challenges are erased, dismissed, or otherwise trampled. The TaNaK (Hebrew scriptures, Old Testament),

113

the Christian Gospels, and the writings of Paul present various statements on divorce, celibacy, gender roles, and marriage. Each passage needs to be examined in terms of both its historical context and its various appropriations by the diverse communities that hold it sacred. If scripture is to be invoked in legislative discussion, the least the public can do is be informed of what the ancient texts say. This point holds for all residents of the United States, regardless of their religious affiliation. The debate typically proceeds according to Christian terms (not unexpectedly, given the Christian majority in the West), but it has a specific valence for Jews, given both the Jewish contexts of Jesus and Paul and the use of Jewish history as a foil for understanding the comments attributed to them.[5]

First, Jesus' views on gender and sexuality inform us Jews of a missing piece of our own history. Jesus was a Jew; his immediate followers were Jews; his views stem from the cultures of Judea and the practices of Judaism. Synagogues and temples too quickly move their educational programs from the Maccabees in the mid-second century B.C.E. to the destruction of the temple in 70 C.E. and then into rabbinic texts. By skipping Christian origins, they sell Jewish history short and fail to recognize the importance of the movements and peoples—pagan, Christian, apocalyptic, etc.—with which, in dialogue and debate, Judaism came to define itself. Concurrently, those congregations that emphasize social justice and *Tikkun Olam* ("mending of the world"), the safety of the State of Israel, and modern midrash, risk losing sight of, or never recognizing, the historical grounding of *Halachah* ("the path one follows, orthopraxy"). We may not agree with those ancient sources, but we should at least know what they say and what the alternatives were.

Second—and this is a major focus of my essay—there is a tendency among Christians and even a few Jews (scholars, theologians, clergy, and laity) to read Jesus' comments on gender and sexuality selectively, and always to the disparagement of Judaism. For example, one of the presenters at a 1994 World Council of Churches seminar asserted: "Two thousand years ago Jesus Christ gave women their rightful place despite the heavy yoke of the Jewish culture weighing on them. For women in general and Jewish women in particular the coming of Jesus meant a revolution."[6]

How revolutionary was Jesus? A few more citations, all from books published by reputable presses within the past ten years, should suffice:

"Christ was the only rabbi who did not discriminate against the women of his time."[7]

And he was needed, given "the dehumanizing situation in which the women of the time were enslaved."[8]

"In Jesus' time, women were not allowed to read scriptures, not allowed to say prayer . . . not allowed to take any form of leadership, not allowed to talk to men in public, not allowed to divorce."[9]

"The honor of the male is . . . based on the sexual purity of the woman related to him (mother, wife, daughters, sisters), not on his own sexual purity. This means that women are confined in inside spaces in the house or the village."[10]

And well she remained there, since "Women in general were believed to be 'gluttonous, eavesdroppers, lazy and jealous,' devoid of intellectual capacity, and living only for self-ornamentation."[11]

In contrast to this monolithically negative social and religious context emerges a Jesus either untouched by or in deliberate rejection of his culture. Jesus' relations with women are seen as "not only innovative, but shocking," because women were "not circumcised and hence could not be part of God's covenant."[12] "As a Jewish rabbi,[13] [Jesus] . . . chose to ignore the traditional Jewish attitudes and instead treated women with compassion and complete acceptance."[14]

To support these views, commentators frequently look to Jesus' pronouncements against divorce; these sayings are then seen as protecting women's honor, saving women from social and economic marginalization, and offering a corrective to a morally degenerate, misogynistic, cruel Judaism: "Jesus explicitly sets about to rectify contemporary ethics, which he sees as debased by Pharisaical Scripture-twisting"[15]; his program was essential, because "Judean divorce practices were particularly unfair to women."[16] He "condemned casual divorce practices in which men took advantage of wives (Mt 19:4–6)."[17] Jesus becomes not only the guardian of family values, but also the savior, in particular, of Jewish women.

These claims are based on a selective reading of rabbinic sources (which should be compared, not to the Gospels, but to the Church Fathers, who are not known either for their "feminist" views); they presume all Jews were wealthy enough to have homes with women's quarters, when in fact this was a luxury only of the very few; they ignore texts—Philo, Josephus, the Pseudepigrapha and the Apocrypha, and the Rabbis—which speak of women's education and intellect, loyalty, prayers, modesty, even divorces. They are, at best, Christian apologetic.

Over twenty years ago, Jewish theologian Judith Plaskow observed that the flip side of Christian feminism is anti-Judaism.[18] Since the evidence that Jesus was specifically concerned with women is confusing (are the elimination of divorce, the emphasis on celibacy, the prioritizing of the movement as opposed to the biological family, good or bad for women?) and possibly negative (e.g., the twelve male apostles in the inner circle, the division of the family home as followers of Jesus take to the road to spread the gospel, the retention of traditional gender roles in parabolic teachings), Christians needed a way to make Jesus look progressive on women's issues. The more misogynistic his first-century Jewish context could be made to appear, the better Jesus looked. The result is both bad history and bad theology, and, unfortunately, public policy draws upon both.

### Divorce and Remarriage: History and Appropriation

The tendency to define Jesus as uniquely progressive on women's issues necessarily affects how commentators interpret his pronouncements on divorce and the family. To explore these topics, the reader must look both to sayings material and to narrative descriptions in the documents of earliest Christianity, and then this information must be correlated with marriage and divorce practices of first-century Jewish society. While the evidence is not entirely consistent for either Jesus or Judaism, a general picture does emerge.

Although Mary Rose D'Angelo cautions that "it can no longer be taken for granted that [the divorce pronouncement] originated with Jesus"[19] and that the legislation may instead derive from early Christian prophecy, I find persuasive the arguments for the authenticity of the divorce legislation attributed to him: multiple sources suggest that Jesus permitted neither divorce nor, especially, marriage after divorce (Mark 10:2–12 [repeated by 1 Cor 7:10–11]; Matt 5:31–32; 19:3–9; and Luke 16:16–18). The prophet Malachi similarly speaks out: "For he hates divorce, says the Lord" (2:16), and divorce is an issue within the Dead Sea Scrolls. Thus, Jesus' sayings are not anomalous.

The majority Jewish view was that divorce and remarriage were permitted; even Malachi's condemnation indicates that the options were available. The debate focused rather on the rationale by which one could obtain a divorce. Given this practical issue, it would not be surprising were someone to have asked Jesus his views.[20]

The Gospels depict Jesus' citing Genesis 2 in support of his radical pronouncement against both divorce and remarriage, and Jesus elsewhere justifies his stances with biblical allusion (e.g., the "sign of Jonah" in Matt 12:39; 16:4; Luke 11:29). Finally, the tradition does attempt to mediate the radicality of the interdiction through both the *porneia* clause in Matt 5:32 and 19:9 and Paul's cautious "if she is separated" (1 Cor 7:11).[21]

I also see little problem with the historicity of Mark's version, even though Mark 10:12—"And if she, having divorced her husband, marries another, she commits adultery"—is typically seen as an adaptation to a gentile setting. Commentators, following rabbinic texts, have assumed that Jewish women in the first century could not sue for divorce. Detailed first-century evidence from Judea and the Galilee is lacking; however, Jewish women in the Diaspora did obtain divorce, and it is quite plausible that Roman culture's somewhat open views on divorce influenced Jewish life under the empire's rule as well.[22] Historians Carolyn Osiek and David Balch observe:

> Divorce was commonly practiced in all ancient Mediterranean societies.... Though it was more likely to be initiated by the husband, a wife too in most situations could initiate divorce, though

sometimes only through the intervention of her father or male relative responsible for protecting her honor and that of her family of origin. Adultery and infertility were the two leading causes of divorce, but there need not be a cause; mutual consent with family approval sufficed.[23]

Finally, I have little trouble in seeing Jesus as extending the definition of adultery to include a sin committed against the first wife by the divorced and remarried husband. Mark 10:11 reads, "Whoever divorces his wife and marries another commits adultery against her." The Torah does not level against a man the charge of adultery were he to have relations with a woman not his wife; he is only forbidden from relations with the wife of another. Thus, Mark 10 offers an intensification of biblical law. Also attesting to the historicity of the intensification is the tradition's attempt to modify its radicality. Matthew 5:32 rewrites the statement: "everyone who divorces his wife . . . makes her an adulteress"; the implication here is that the first wife's remarriage would be adulterous. Matthew 19:3–12 and Luke 16:18 omit the sin against the wife.

Jesus forbade divorce and, especially, remarriage to both husband and wife. This is an egalitarian move, not in its providing women new legal options but in its placing women and men in the same position: neither should divorce or remarry. However, scholars debate both the causes and the benefits (especially to women) of this innovation.

The standard response conjoins the two debates. Scholars argue that Jewish men were, willy nilly, leaving their wives without resources, honor, or hope: "for centuries prior to the time of Christ, men had developed their patriarchal privilege to include the putting away of their wives for trivial reasons, even for spoiling a dish, according to Hillel."[24] (The rabbinic reference is M. Gittin 9.10.) Jesus, then, sought to protect women from such systemic abuse. This construct connects him with those present-day organizations that want to strengthen families by instituting covenantal marriage, restricting divorce, and otherwise legislating "family values" in an increasingly decadent society.

The argument is, however, wrong. First, there is no evidence of rampant divorce in the first century. M. Gittin 9.10 (cf. Sifre Deut 269), which also cites R. Akiva's claim that a man could divorce "even if he found someone else prettier than she" is not indicative of social fact; it is rabbinic rhetoric intended to show what is possible given certain legal presuppositions. It is no more descriptive of second temple Jewish society than is Jesus' exhortation to pluck out the offending eye and chop off the offending hand indicative of a group of blind and maimed messianists. In addition, while Christian scholars show little hesitation in citing Akiva's statement, rarely do they look in the Mishnah. Akiva's comment itself responds to the House of Shammai's restriction of divorce to cases of unchastity (citing Deut 24:1; cf. Matthew's *porneia* clause). Moreover, in response to Akiva, the Talmud cites R. Eliezer: "Whoever divorces his first wife, the very altar sheds tears for him" (*B. Sanhedrin* 22a).[25]

Second, we do not have an indication that divorce left either the man or the woman without honor; because the marital relationship was treated as a contract, divorce was, at least according to the system, no more implicated in shame than would be the termination of a contract for services. As Osiek and Balch state, divorce in antiquity "usually did not carry with it any noticeable form of social stigma."[26] The divorcée was then free to remarry, and likely many did.

Third, Jewish women received marriage contracts (*Kethubot*; singular, *Ketubhah*), which made divorce financially prohibitive for the husband and guaranteed the wife some financial security should the marriage be dissolved.[27] Tal Ilan observes that "the number of actual documented cases of divorce during the [second temple] period is relatively small. . . . The main reason for the paucity of actual cases seems to be economic: divorce was very expensive for the man, who had to pay his former wife her *Ketubhah*, for which all his property was accountable."[28]

Finally, since polygamy was permitted to Jewish men, divorce was not necessary in cases of a man's "finding someone prettier," as R. Akiva put it.

Certainly, some divorces may have functioned to the detriment of the woman; some may have involved false charges causing her to lose not only her *Ketubhah* but also her honor, but these need not be seen as normative. Nor would requiring a loveless marriage to continue necessarily be to the wife's benefit.

Most of the evidence for Jewish divorce in the first century comes from the elite classes: Josephus (*Ant.* 20:143–47) recounts the separations of Agrippa I's daughters Bernice (from Polemo of Cilicia), Drusilla (from Azizus of Emesa), and Mariamne (from Julius Archelaus). He also speaks (*Life* 415) of how his first wife left him. *Antiquities* 15.259 mentions that Herod's sister Salome sent her second husband, Costobarus, a bill of divorce. Regarding the best-known divorce in the Gospels, Ilan remarks: "Herodias acted as a fully empowered party in the cancellation of her marriage with Herod the son of Herod and her subsequent marriage to his high-ranking brother, Antipas" (*Ant.* 18.110).[29] Although Josephus insists that among the Jews, "It is only the man who is permitted by us" to divorce (*Ant.* 15.259), his comment is questionable in that he continues by anomalously (and probably incorrectly) observing that a divorced woman requires her ex-husband's permission to remarry; plausibly he is attempting to paint a picture for his gentile readers of Judaism's moral (i.e., patriarchal) superiority.

The Gospel of Matthew depicts Joseph who, "being a righteous man and not wanting to disgrace [Mary], planned to divorce her secretly" (1:19) upon finding her pregnant. The divorce appears then to be a *Halachic* response to Mary's (ostensibly) breaking her marriage contract. That Joseph could divorce "secretly" or "quietly" both complements his righteousness (he does not seek her public humiliation) and demonstrates that divorce need not lead to scandal.[30]

Thus, the historical evidence counters claims that situate Jesus' forbidding of divorce in the context of a Jewish society in which divorce was rampant and divorcées were left destitute. To understand Jesus' injunction, a source other than a hypothetical societal ill, and an approach other than anti-Jewish apologetic, needs to be discovered.

### The New Family of the Disciples

Jesus' views concerning divorce and remarriage should fit within his overall message. However, publications on Christian marriage and divorce typically do not focus on Jesus' overall mission and message;

rather, they list the various biblical pronouncements, offer little if any explanation for Jesus' statements (other than positing the negative view of Judaism described above), and then either focus on subsequent church-historical discussions or provide pastoral guidance.

Studies of Jesus, on the other hand, typically do not look in detail at his comments on divorce and remarriage. Nor, indeed, do the majority of constructs of Jesus have a place within which to contextualize these comments. Neither Jesus the "Cynic sage" nor Jesus the "compassionate visionary" provides an adequate context for understanding the divorce statements. The only view of Jesus' program that does make sense of the radical pronouncements is that of eschatological prophet.[31] In the context of millenarian piety, family configurations change. A strong sexual ethic is often the hallmark of apocalyptic communities (1 Corinthians and Revelation are instructive), as is the attempt to recreate the golden age.[32] The divorce legislation conforms to all these characteristics.

Mark's Jesus provides an atemporal frame for his injunctions against divorce:

> Because of your hardness of heart, [Moses] wrote this command-ment [concerning the mechanism of divorce] for you. But from the beginning of creation, "God made them male and female." For this reason, a man shall leave his father and mother and be joined to his wife, and the two shall become one flesh. So they are no longer two, but one flesh. Therefore, what God has joined together, let no one separate. (Mark 10:2–12; cf. Gen 1:27; 2:24)

The appeal to Genesis, to the golden age, is typical of millenarian piety.

As an intensification of traditional practices, Mark 10:2–12 is not contrary to *Halakhah* (cf. Deut 24:1); there is no law requiring one to divorce. It is, rather, an intensification of Torah based on Torah itself. A similar argument, in the context of another, biblically based ideal, is found in the Dead Sea Scrolls. These texts clearly legislate against polygamy (11QTemple 57:17–19 includes the statement, "He shall take no other wife apart from [his first wife]") and may well speak against remarriage after divorce or the death of a spouse (see CD 4:21–5:6

[esp. 4:19–21]: ". . . are caught twice in fornication by taking two wives in their lives, even though the principle of creation is 'male and female he created them'").[33]

Within an eschatological context, family dynamics necessarily shift. Luke 18:29 reads, "Truly I tell you, there is no one who has left house *or wife* or brothers or parents or children, for the sake of the kingdom of God, who will not get back very much more in this age, and in the age to come eternal life" (italics added; see also Luke 14:20, 26; 20:34–36). While most commentators assume Luke added "wife" (it is missing from Mark 10:29–30 and Matt 19:29), perhaps the other Evangelists omitted the reference, since "to leave a wife" can also connote "to divorce" (see 1 Cor 7:11).[34] Separation in the context of millenarian piety, while refusing divorce, is not unusual (for example, the Shakers). Such movements do not want to risk sexual scandal: members are not to use their affiliation in order to justify either divorce or remarriage.

Whether Jesus endorsed marriage is a separate and equally conflicted question. Within the synoptic tradition, marriage functions primarily as a metaphor. Jesus is the bridegroom, but there is no bride (see Matthew's Parable of the Ten Virgins, 25:1–13); he occupies the liminal position between being single and being a husband. The impact of the metaphor is one of joyful anticipation and celebration, but there is no consummation. Most of the people he encounters appear apart from typical domestic arrangements; the only married couple who appear together, aside from the deadly relationship of Herodias and Antipas (Mark 6:14–19; Matt 14:1–12) is the (synagogue) ruler and his wife (Matt 9:18–26; Mark 5:21–43; Luke 8:40–56).

Jesus' statement that the married couple become "one flesh" does appear to endorse both marriage and the sexuality attendant to it (Matt 19:5; Mark 10:7). Yet even this ostensibly simple statement is complicated. The tradition also appears to commend celibacy: Jesus speaks also of "eunuchs for the kingdom of Heaven" (Matt 19:12) and, as noted above, he speaks of the importance of owing him, not the spouse, loyalty. Perhaps then his reference to "one flesh" is an evangelistic addition that extends a shorter, earlier biblical allusion. Perhaps it is less an endorsement of sexual intercourse than it is of the new family related not biologically or by contract, but by loyalty to Jesus.[35] Granted, these ideas are highly speculative, but they do provide at least two cogent means of understanding the various pronouncements.

In John's Gospel, the matter becomes much more indeterminate: Jesus is not only present at the wedding in Cana, he also provides excellent wine. He also finds an evangelist in a much-married woman from Samaria. However, many biblical scholars question the historicity of both accounts. They are otherwise unattested in the Gospel tradition. Jesus typically does not do miracles for self-serving reasons. John's stories tend to emphasize symbolic rather than literal meanings, and Jesus elsewhere eschews travel to Samaria and even contact with Samaritans (Matt 10:5b; Luke 9:51–56).

Yet even if we take both Johannine accounts as historical, we may still have a Jesus who favors celibacy. Attendance at a wedding is no more an endorsement of marriage than eating at the home of a tax collector or sinner is an endorsement of tax collecting or sin. Jesus provides the wine as a favor for his mother; he is never shown in contact with the bride and groom. While Jesus does not condemn the Samaritan woman, neither does he praise her multiple marriages and present cohabitation; moreover, her encounter with Jesus occurs not when she is married, but when she is with a man who is not her husband. For Jesus, the ideal state is apparently that of the single person, the person who does not procreate (Matthew 19's "eunuchs for the kingdom"), the person who is like the angels in heaven, who "neither marry nor are given in marriage" (Luke 20:34–36, cf. Mark 12:24–25; Matt 22:30).

If Jesus is, like Paul and, apparently, like John the Baptist, convinced that a new way of living is around the corner, then it makes a great deal of sense for him to construct a fictive kinship group or a countercultural view of marriage and the family. That is, if one believes the end of the world is imminent, one is, so cross-cultural studies tell us, much more likely either to intensify marital relationships by forbidding divorce (thereby recreating the golden age), or to erase all law and live in sexual freedom.[36] Jesus chose the former.

124 • Amy-Jill Levine

## The Next Generations

Judaism, as it came to be formulated through rabbinic thought, pre-served the option of divorce, encouraged its practitioners to "be fruit-ful and multiply," and determined voluntary celibacy to be an oddity. The Pauline churches, and likely Paul himself, saw celibacy as the preferable lifestyle. Complementing the reference to Gen 1:27 in the Jesus tradition, Gal 3:28 speaks of how in Christ there is "not male and not female"; that is, the new creation is like the earthling (ha-adam) prior to the creation of the one into two, male and female.[37]

For Mark, marriage may have functioned as a form of "sacrificial service," and therefore as a form of discipleship.[38] Retaining Jesus' escha-tological interests, Mark insists that there is to be no divorce. Matthew's Gospel offers an adaptation of the injunction: the Matthean Jesus per-mits, if not actually requires, divorce in the case of *porneia*. Luke adapts the prohibition against remarriage into a general program of asceticism. For example, Luke 20:34–36 affirms that "those who belong to this age marry and are given in marriage, but those who are considered worthy of a place in that age and in the resurrection from the dead neither marry nor are given in marriage" (see also Matt 22:30; Mark 12:25). Aside from the infancy narratives, the only extended account of a mar-ried couple in Luke's corpus is that of Ananias and Sapphira (Acts 5:1–11); their example is not a strong endorsement of marital benefits.

Outside the Gospels, Christian scripture continued to adapt. While Rev 14:4 commends the 144,000 male virgins "who have not defiled themselves with women," 1 Tim 2:15 insists that women gain salvation through childbearing. Some communities, for example, those attested by the apocryphal Acts, moved toward monastic models; still others, represented by Ephesians and the Pastoral Epistles (1–2 Timothy, Titus), subscribed to the household codes of Roman patriarchal society.

It is the genius of the Church that it applied its "prophetic authority to understand, apply, rethink, even suppress the prohibitions [against divorce] in response to their own situations."[39] How much more adapt-ing it does, in light not just of current moves to liberalism[40] but also in light of both what may be concluded about Jesus' own historical con-text and the real problems of real people, remains to be seen. The most convincing historical case I can make for Jesus locates him as eschato-logically motivated: something was about to change, either through war, or divine intervention into history. Like John before him and Paul after him, Jesus saw the importance of dedicating one's life to the *basileia* (kingdom). Marriage and children are distractions at best, likely signs of the weakness of the flesh, and soon to pass away as we all become angels in heaven. He did not approve of divorce, and his dis-approval of remarriage was even greater.

Today we tend to plan for the future. Given this shift, adaptations to the radicality of Jesus' pronouncements are necessary: for battered spouses who will more likely see the end of their life than the end of the world if they remain in the marriage; for relationships that have dis-solved into a miasma which condemns not only husband and wife but also children; and for the divorced or widowed who seek remarriage for love, companionship, economic stability, and wholeness. Jesus did not speak to these issues, although the Jewish tradition that followed upon his time period does, as do many churches established in his name.

Finally, whatever Jesus said, the canon of the Church offers several options. This theological point should not be lost on those who adduce only select statements to establish policy. Individuals most likely to appeal to Jesus are also often likely to subscribe to a biblical literalism. Ironically, they only cite those portions of the text that support their preconceptions. Those who insist on the legal necessity of preserving marriages marked by incompatibility, desertion, and abuse have yet, as far as I am aware, to demonstrate their own fidelity to the words of the gospel by plucking out their own offending eyes and cutting off their own offending hands, making themselves eunuchs for the *basileia*, sell-ing all they have and giving to the poor, and turning the other cheek.

NOTES

1. This essay is based on a talk given to the Hillsboro Presbyterian Church in Nashville (October 1997) and the priests of the Middle Tennessee Diocese of the Roman Catholic Church (November 1997). I thank both groups for their thoughtful questions and trenchant suggestions. For a complementary paper

that, in addition to divorce, explores Jesus' views on celibacy and gender roles in relation to his Jewish social matrix, see Amy-Jill Levine, "The Word Becomes Flesh: Jesus, Gender, and Sexuality," in Florida Southern Biblical Symposium series, ed. Walter Weaver and James Charlesworth (Harrisburg, Pa.: Trinity Press International, 2000).

2. See Sheila R. Kennedy, *Shattered Faith* (New York: Pantheon, 1997).

3. See Irving A. Breitowitz, *Between Civil and Religious Law: The Plight of the Agunah in American Society* (Westport, Conn.: Greenwood, 1993); Jack N. Porter, ed., *Women in Chains: A Sourcebook on the Agunah* (Northvale, Ill.: Jason Aronson, 1996).

4. See Joshua Harris, *I Kissed Dating Good-Bye: A New Attitude toward Romance and Relationships* (Sisters, Ore.: Multnomah Publishers, 1997).

5. Pauline materials are beyond the scope of this essay. For general information on the use of Judaism as a negative foil for Pauline thought, see the now classic: E. P. Sanders, *Paul and Palestinian Judaism* (London: SCM Press, 1977), esp. 1–29.

6. Marguérite Fassinou, "Challenges for Feminist Theology in Francophone Africa," in *Women's Visions: Theological Reflection, Celebration, Action*, ed. Ofelia Ortega (Geneva: WCC Publications, 1995), 9. On the origins of and corrections to such anti-Jewish material in international women's scholarship, including the several examples cited below, see Amy-Jill Levine, "Lilies of the Field and Wandering Jews: Biblical Scholarship, Women's Roles, and Social Location," in *Transformative Encounters. Jesus and Women Re-viewed*, ed. Ingrid-Rosa Kitzberger (Leiden: E. J. Brill, 2000).

7. Grace Eneme, "Living Stones," in *New Eyes for Reading: Biblical and Theological Reflections by Women from the Third World*, ed. John S. Pobee and Bärbel von Wartenberg-Potter (Geneva: WCC Publications, 1986), 30. Her example of "nondiscrimination" is that Jesus "allowed Susanna, Joanna and others to minister with him."

8. Hisako Kinukawa, "A Well-Cherished but Much-Clouded Story," in *Reading from this Place*, vol. 2, *Social Location and Biblical Interpretation in Global Perspective*, ed. Fernando F. Segovia and Mary Ann Tolbert (Minneapolis: Fortress Press, 1995), 85.

9. Alina Maente Machema, "Jumping Culture's Fences," in *Talitha, Qumi! Proceedings of the Convocation of African Women Theologians*, ed. Mercy Amba Oduyoye and Musimbi Kanyoro (Ibadan, Nigeria: Daystar, 1990), 133.

10. Hisako Kinukawa, *Women and Jesus in Mark: A Japanese Feminist Perspective*, The Bible and Liberation Series (Maryknoll, N.Y.: Orbis Books, 1994), 12.

11. This is but a sample (citing *Genesis Rabbah*) of the description of Jewish women from Teresa Okure, "Women in the Bible," in *With Passion and Compassion: Third World Women Doing Theology*, ed. Virginia Fabella and Mercy A. Oduyoye (Maryknoll, N.Y.: Orbis Books, 1988), 103.

12. María Clara Bingemer, "Reflections on the Trinity," in *Through Her Eyes: Women's Theology from Latin America*, ed. Elsa Tamez (Maryknoll, N.Y.: Orbis

Books, 1989), 71, citing Leonardo Boff, *The Maternal Face of God: The Feminine and Its Religious Expressions* (San Francisco: Harper & Row, 1987), 81. Jewish women, it should go without saying, are part of the covenant, as both those by birth and those by choice could then, and do now, attest.

13. A frequent tautology.

14. Bette Ekeye, "Woman, For How Long Not?" in *Feminist Theology from the Third World: A Reader*, ed. Ursula King (London: SPCK; Maryknoll, N.Y.: Orbis Books, 1994), 145.

15. William F. Luck, *Divorce and Remarriage: Recovering the Biblical View* (San Francisco: Harper & Row, 1987), 86. George R. Ewald, *Jesus and Divorce: A Biblical Guide for Ministry to Divorced Persons* (Waterloo, Ont: Herald, 1991) begins with a "brief review of Jewish marriage customs and abuses of patriarchal rights" (p. 21) against which he contrasts the "gentler, more sensitive" 1 Timothy.

16. John Temple Bristow, *What the Bible Really Says about Love, Marriage, and the Family* (St. Louis, Mo.: Chalice Press, 1994), 111.

17. Walter A. Elwell and Robert W. Yarbrough, *Encountering the New Testament: A Historical and Theological Survey* (Grand Rapids: Baker Book House, 1998), 341. I cite this volume in particular because it is becoming the most common textbook in evangelical classrooms. Matthew 19:4–6, by the way, says nothing about "casual practices" or "taking advantage of wives."

18. Judith Plaskow, "Blaming the Jews for the Birth of Patriarchy," *Lilith* 7 (fall 1980): 11–12, 14–17; Judith Plaskow, "Anti-Judaism in Feminist Christian Interpretation," in *Searching the Scriptures*, vol. 1, *A Feminist Introduction*, ed. Elisabeth Schüssler Fiorenza (New York: Crossroad, 1993), 117–29. See also Susannah Heschel, "Anti-Judaism in Christian Feminist Theology," *Tikkun* 5.3 (May-June 1990): 25–28, 95–97; Amy-Jill Levine, "Yeast of Eden: Jesus, Second Temple Judaism, and Women," *Biblical Interpretation* 2 (March 1994): 8–33; Levine, "Lilies of the Field."

19. Mary Rose D'Angelo, "Remarriage and the Divorce Sayings Attributed to Jesus," in *Divorce and Remarriage*, ed. William G. Roberts (Kansas City, Mo.: Sheed & Ward, 1990), 93.

20. N. T. Wright, *Jesus and the Victory of God* (Minneapolis: Fortress Press, 1996), 397–98, suggests that the teaching in Mark 10:10 is cryptic, given the political liability of arguing against divorce in Antipas's territory; cf. Mark 6:18, 21–29.

21. The Greek term *porneia* has a broad semantic range, much as does its derivative, "pornography." *Porneia* may concern marriages rendered illegal by consanguinity (Lev 18:6–18); divorce would then be warranted. This argument receives support from both Matthew's respect for Torah and the connection of *porneia* to gentile catechumens in Acts 15:20, 29; 21:25. A second explanation is that Matthew's clause, like the *Shepherd of Hermas*, reflects the Roman legislation of 18 B.C.E. (the *lex iulia de adulteriis*) making adultery a crime, such that the man who did not divorce and prosecute his adulterous wife could be accused of pimping (*lenocinium*). Even if *porneia* be given its most broad definition of "sexual misconduct" and therefore seen to include not only adultery and incest but also

intercourse during menstruation, homosexual encounters, visiting prostitutes, and other behaviors condemned in various parts of scripture, it is unlikely that Jesus added the reference to *porneia*. In Jewish settings, incestuous marriage would be illegal in the first place; in Jesus' announcement of the *basileia*, escape clauses are as rare as camels that can fit through needles' eyes.

22. See Bernadette Brooten, "Konnten Frauen in altem Judentum die Scheidung betrieben? Überlegungen zu Mk 10, 11–12 und 1 Kor 7, 10–11," *Evangelische Theologie* 42 (January–February 1982): 65–80; Bernadette Brooten, "Zur Debatte über das Scheidungsrecht der jüdischen Frau," *Evangelische Theologie* 43 (September–October 1983): 466–78. On Jewish marriage contracts from antiquity, in which the wife is accorded the ability to stipulate divorce proceedings, see Mordecai Friedman, *Jewish Marriage in Palestine*, 2 vols. (Tel Aviv: Jewish Theological Seminary, 1980), vol. 1, chap. 5, and see also discussion in Rachel Adler, *Engendering Judaism: An Inclusive Theology and Ethics* (Boston: Beacon Press, 1998), 178–80.

23. Carolyn Osiek and David Balch, *Families in the New Testament World*, The Family, Religion, and Culture Series (Louisville, Ky.: Westminster John Knox Press, 1997), 62.

24. Ewald, *Jesus and Divorce*, 18.

25. See the discussion in Tal Ilan, *Jewish Women in Greco-Roman Palestine* (Peabody, Mass.: Hendrickson Publishers, 1996), 141–47.

26. Osiek and Balch, *Families in the New Testament World*, 62.

27. See John J. Collins, "Marriage, Divorce, and Family in Second Temple Judaism," in *Families in Ancient Israel*, ed. L. G. Perdue et al., The Family, Religion, and Culture Series (Louisville, Ky.: Westminster John Knox Press, 1997), 107–12, 115–19.

28. Ilan, *Jewish Women*, 147. The number of papyri attesting to divorce does rise for the Bar Kokhba period. See the review of Ilan by John J. Collins in *Journal of Religion* 77 (January 1997): 123–25.

29. Ilan, *Jewish Women*, 80.

30. The second-century Christian document *Shepherd of Hermas* (4.1.4–12) requires divorce in the case of adultery. The husband is then forbidden to remarry. The Jewish pseudepigraphon *Slavonic (2) Enoch* 71 depicts the decision of Noah's brother, Nir, to divorce his wife upon finding her pregnant and knowing that he is not the father.

31. See E. P. Sanders, *The Historical Figure of Jesus* (London: Penguin Books, 1993), 198, on "perfectionism and the new age"; cf. E. P. Sanders, *Jesus and Judaism* (Philadelphia: Fortress Press, 1985), 256–60. Sanders cautions that the divorce saying does not "prove that Jesus' world-view was determined by eschatological expectation" (*Jesus and Judaism*, 259). I argue the reverse: eschatological expectation makes the best sense of the injunction.

32. Wright, *Jesus and the Victory*, 285–87, connects the injunction with Jesus' vision of the "new heart" and the inauguration of the "new covenant."

33. For the texts, see Florentino García Martínez, *The Dead Sea Scrolls Translated*, 2d ed (Leiden: E. J. Brill, 1996), 174, 36. Geza Vermes, "Sectarian Matrimonial Halakhah in the Damascus Rule," *Journal of Jewish Studies* 25 (February 1974): 197–202, insists that the scrolls prohibit not divorce but polygamy.

34. D'Angelo, "Remarriage and the Divorce Sayings," 95.

35. See the discussion, with references, in Andrew Cornes, *Divorce and Remarriage: Biblical Principles and Pastoral Care* (Grand Rapids: Wm. B. Eerdmans Publishing, 1993), 58–61. Geoffrey Robinson, *Marriage, Divorce and Nullity: A Guide to the Annulment Process in the Catholic Church* (Collegeville, Minn.: Liturgical Press, 1987), 69, nicely states: "A married couple can no more cease to be husband and wife than a brother and sister can cease to be brother and sister."

36. Possibly Jesus viewed intercourse and hence semen production as a necessary evil that brought about weakness and loss of spiritual vigor; such a view was common in Mediterranean society. See Osiek and Balch, *Families in the New Testament World*, 104–7.

37. See D'Angelo, "Remarriage and the Divorce Sayings," 101.

38. Richard B. Hays, *The Moral Vision of the New Testament: A Contemporary Introduction to New Testament Ethics* (San Francisco: HarperSanFrancisco, 1996), 350. Hays suggests Mark likely "radicalized" a saying of Jesus that forbade remarriage after divorce (cf. Matt 5:31–32; Luke 16:18): Hays, *Moral Vision*, 352.

39. D'Angelo, "Remarriage and the Divorce Sayings," 79. For thorough treatments of interpretations of the various pronouncements, see William A. Heth and Gordon J. Wenham, *Jesus and Divorce: Towards an Evangelical Understanding of New Testament Teaching* (London: Hodder & Stoughton, 1984); Theodore Mackin, *Divorce and Remarriage: Marriage in the Catholic Church* (Ramsey, N.J.: Paulist Press, 1984). Mackin's 565 pages, which could have been extended with more detailed exegesis of the Gospels, indicate how complicated, and controversial, the question is.

40. Cornes, *Divorce and Remarriage*, is refreshingly consistent in insisting that remarriage is illegitimate. I am relieved he is not my pastor.

# 7. JESUS OF HOLLYWOOD
## A Jewish Perspective
*Adele Reinhartz*

According to the synoptic tradition, Jesus of Nazareth was vitally con-
cerned with popular perception. "Who do people say that I am?" asks
Jesus of his disciples (Mark 8:27). The disciples answer, "John the
Baptist; and others say, Elijah; and others one of the prophets."
Apparently not satisfied, Jesus asks them, "But who do you say that I
am?" Peter answers him, "You are the Christ" (Mark 8:27–29).[1]

The variety of opinions regarding who Jesus was implies widespread
popular awareness of Jesus in first-century Palestine; the general silence
of the Jewish and Roman literature implies the contrary. But to the
extent that there were popular perceptions of Jesus, we may imagine
that these were mediated through personal encounter, up close or at a
distance, at formal sermons or by word of mouth, rumors, and gossip.
Twenty centuries and many miles removed from Jesus' original context,
however, there is no doubt that Jesus enjoys, or perhaps laments from
some heavenly vantage point, extremely high popular recognition,
among Christians and non-Christians alike.  Popular perceptions of
Jesus in our own time and place are mediated both through verbal
communication—sermons and lectures, for example—and through
other forms such as art, music, drama, and literature including the texts
of the New Testament itself. But arguably the most powerful, and the
most problematic, medium shaping our perceptions of Jesus is film.

Jesus' cinematic appearances can be divided into three categories,
those in which he appears as himself, as in *The Greatest Story Ever Told*
(1965) or *Jesus of Nazareth* (1977); those in which he appears indirectly,
through a Jesus-like redeemer figure, as in *Cool Hand Luke* (1967) and
*Shawshank Redemption* (1994); and those in which he appears as the

subject of study, as in the recent PBS documentary, *From Jesus to Christ* (1998). This essay focuses on films in the first category, which provide a variety of answers to Jesus' urgent question, "Who do people say that I am?"

The cinematic Jesus has come under considerable scrutiny, though not quite as much as his scriptural counterpart. A recent spate of books and articles survey the Jesus films with respect to their overall characterization of Jesus, their aesthetic merit, and their reception on the part of Christian and non-Christian viewers and reviewers.[2] My own interest in Jesus of Hollywood is more specific. As a New Testament scholar, I am curious to see how and whether these celluloid representations of Jesus—who the filmmakers say he is—relates to the academic portraits of Jesus, that is, who scholars say he is. As a Jewish New Testament scholar, however, my interest in both the scholarship and the movies is focused specifically on one aspect of Jesus' characterization, namely, his identity as a Jew. My interest in this question is not merely academic. It is also fueled by a conviction that the cinematic representations of Jesus both reflect and also affect cultural perceptions of both Jesus and Judaism.

That Jesus was a Jew might seem so obvious as to warrant little discussion. Given the unanimity of the New Testament, New Testament scholars have no choice but to concur.[3] Filmmakers seem similarly convinced of Jesus' Jewish identity. This unusual consensus is deceptive, however. Upon further probing it becomes apparent that the claim that Jesus was a Jew has a different content and significance within each of the Jesus portraits, whether scholarly or cinematic.

For E. P. Sanders, Geza Vermes, Séan Freyne, Paula Fredriksen, and a host of other Christian and Jewish scholars, Jesus' Jewishness is central to their construction of his identity and earthly career.[4] These scholars picture Jesus as a Jew like most of those around him in Galilee. He observed both the ritual and the ethical requirements of the law,[5] including the laws of Sabbath, purity, sacrifice and atonement.[6] His teachings were similar to those of the Pharisees,[7] and he subscribed fully to the notions of election and Torah. Most important to Jesus' mission were eschatology and apocalyptic thinking, which led him to see and portray himself as a prophet of the eschaton. He foresaw an end to the current world order when God would step in to create a radically new order. Like other prophets before him, he strongly protested what he saw as the corruption of true worship in the temple and hence both spoke and acted against the priests who had authority there.[8] In this model, Jesus, and Jesus scholars, have a positive attitude toward Judaism. Jesus is situated firmly within a Jewish context that bears a strong resemblance to rabbinic Judaism and indeed remains familiar within the framework of traditional Judaism today.

This scholarly portrait has its cinematic counterpart in Zeffirelli's lengthy television epic, *Jesus of Nazareth*, released in 1977. This film blends or harmonizes the four Gospels and amplifies their material considerably. Widely considered to be the best Jesus film in the harmonizing genre,[9] *Jesus of Nazareth* expresses Zeffirelli's conviction that Jesus was a Jew, probably a Pharisee, immersed in the most Jewish practices and customs imaginable.[10] Zeffirelli's Jesus holds to the central Jewish understanding of election, scripture, and messianism,[11] and does not set himself apart from the Pharisees, though they occasionally object to the company that he keeps, such as Matthew the tax collector and Mary Magdalene. This understanding of Jesus' Jewishness is apparent both directly, through the words and deeds attributed to Jesus, and indirectly, for example, through the portrayal of Joseph with side curls reminiscent of certain orthodox Jewish groups today.[12] It is also indicated in the lavish depiction of the Galilean Jewish setting, and in particular, in the many synagogue scenes that depict Jewish rituals utilizing familiar prayers in English and Hebrew. These scenes resonate with the contemporary Jewish liturgy without precisely duplicating it. In the opening scene, for example, the rabbi reads from a scroll, replaces it in the ark, and recites the priestly blessing (Num 6:24–27). In the background to Jesus' circumcision is the central prayer known as the *Sh'ma* ("Hear O Israel, the Lord thy God the Lord is One;" Deut 6:4) chanted in Hebrew. Zeffirelli's Jesus comes to fulfill the eschatological hopes of a downtrodden people whose despair is expressed in biblical terms. For example, the scene highlighting the Jews' grief in the aftermath of the Romans' slaughter of the innocents (Matt 1:16–18) is followed by the return of Mary, Joseph, and the infant Jesus to Nazareth (Matt 1:19–20), as it is in Matthew's Gospel. But the visual juxtaposition of the death scene in Bethlehem and the pastoral landscape of Galilee, and the abrupt change in musical soundtrack from dirge-like to cheerful, accentuate the implied message that Jesus is God's response to the Jews' lament.

A second scholarly trend in the current quest of the historical Jesus focuses not on what was specific to Galilean Judaism but rather on the features that Galilean Jews shared with other groups in the Mediterranean area. Jesus' pithy sayings and aphoristic social critique resemble in form and content the "wit and wisdom of the wandering Cynic sage."[13] Like gentile Cynics, Jesus and his disciples traveled light, lived on the road, and challenged others to live as they did. Jesus' message may have been more communally oriented than that of the gentile Cynics, and he may have frequented rural rather than the urban areas in which gentile Cynics operated, but otherwise there was little to distinguish between them.[14] For Jesus the Jewish cynic, the kingdom was not a future cataclysmic event but was present now in the quality of people's relations with one another. His willingness to eat with sinners and touch the sick was a direct challenge to the laws, mores, and social boundaries of common Judaism. Jesus' message was symbolized above all in his opposition to the temple.[15] This opposition, however, is not to be construed as eschatological in any way. The Cynic hypothesis does not deny Jesus' Jewishness but rather argues that his placement in first-century Galilee and his Jewish identity did not keep him from being critical of, or even unconcerned with, certain aspects of his culture, including religious ones.[16]

The Cynic option is not taken up directly by any of the Jesus films that I viewed. But two key aspects of this hypothesis, that Jesus was not overly concerned with the specifics of Jewish religious thought and practice, and that Jesus' message was not primarily eschatological or apocalyptic, can be seen in Martin Scorsese's *Last Temptation of Christ* (1988). This film does not claim to be a story of the historical Jesus, but rather an adaptation of Nikos Kazantzakis's novel of the same name. Nevertheless, it is a Jesus story of sorts, and invites comparison with the other Jesus films.[17] *Last Temptation* situates Jesus in first-century

Palestine. It focuses, however, not on Jesus' objective historical and spiritual identity, but on the inner struggle between the demands of God and the temptations of the flesh. This central theme is made explicit in the quotation from Kazantzakis's novel that precedes the title frame: "The dual substance of Christ—the yearning so human, so superhuman, of man to attain God ... has always been a deep inscrutable mystery to me. My principle [sic] anguish and source of all my joys and sorrows from my youth onward has been the incessant, merciless battle between the spirit and the flesh ... and my soul is the arena where these two armies have clashed and met." For Scorcese, Jesus' crucifixion does not mark the advent of the kingdom, but rather Jesus' personal resolution of the conflict between spirit and flesh. This movie focuses on the universal human dilemma rather than a particular historical conflict or its theological ramifications. Although there is no explicit reference to the Cynic peasant theory, Jesus himself does look rather peasant-like as he and his followers wander around the countryside.[18]

An even stronger statement of Jesus' affinity with the peasant class is made in Pier Paolo Pasolini's *The Gospel According to St. Matthew* (1995), in which Jesus and his disciples resemble the downtrodden populace in their dress and hairstyle, and are sharply distinguished in appearance from the Romans on the one hand and the Jewish authorities on the other hand. Pasolini's Jesus, too, roams the countryside, stopping occasionally to teach and preach to his disciples and the population at large.

The third scholarly model, represented by Marcus Borg and N. T. Wright, pictures Jesus in decidedly antinationalist terms.[19] While acknowledging that Jesus used apocalyptic language, this model argues that such language was understood metaphorically rather than literally.[20] Jesus was a prophet engaged in radical social criticism expressed through his opposition to the temple-centered purity-obsessed society and through his practice of inclusive table fellowship. His vision was the formation of an alternative community that sought to live in history under the kingship of God. But the kingdom of God was not an eschatological construct. Rather, it was expected here on earth in the time-space world.[21] In contrast to other leaders within Jewish Palestine, who engaged in the politics of purity, Jesus preached and lived the politics of compassion.[22] Jesus called Israel away from the rules of Deuteronomy, which had been only a temporary phase in God's purposes, and he acted out against the temple, which was the symbol of Judaism's violent nationalism.[23]

Some affinities exist between the antinationalist Jesus described by Borg and Wright and the Jesus as depicted in Denis Arcand's *Jesus of Montreal* (1989). Arcand's movie, as the title implies, is set in modern-day Montreal. It features a small troupe of underemployed actors who are hired by the priest of St. Joseph's oratory, a major religious site on the peak of Mount Royal, to revitalize the tired Passion Play that has been performed there for years. The result is a powerful new play that presents a Jesus so vital and compelling that at least one member of the audience believes him to be real.

The Passion Play asserts emphatically that Jesus was a Jew. But this assertion is given little content in either the Passion Play itself or the frame narrative in which it is embedded. Within this frame narrative, the actors become involved in the drama of their own lives, which mirrors the characters, content, and structure of the Passion Play that they perform. In the modern-day frame narrative, acts and words that echo the Gospels become symbolic of contemporary issues. Daniel Coulombe, the actor who plays Jesus in the Passion Play, overturns the tables and shatters the high-tech equipment of those who have turned the theater into a vulgar temple to the advertising industry when Mireille—the play's Mary Magdalene—is asked to bare her breasts in an audition for a beer commercial. Just as Jesus is offered the kingdoms of the world and their splendors in exchange for worshiping Satan (Matt 4:9), so is Daniel offered a tempting glimpse of power and wealth by a smooth-talking lawyer in a tall tower overlooking downtown Montreal. At Daniel's death, caused when the cross to which he is strapped at the climax of the Passion Play topples, his corneas and heart are transplanted into others, giving literal meaning to the notion that Jesus is the source of new sight and renewed life.

These events and many others like them require a symbolic interpretation of the seminal actions of Jesus in the Gospels. The confrontation with Satan is an indictment of contemporary values rather than a struggle with a powerful, superhuman adversary. The cleansing of the temple is not a prelude to, or a symbol of, the coming eschatological crisis but a protest against the exploitation of women and the exaltation of crass commercialism. The resurrection is not the promise of eternal life for those who believe but a healing of the physical body through the miracle of modern medicine and the generosity of Daniel/Jesus' companions. Symbol, metaphor, and allegory reign supreme.

The cinematic parallels to these three scholarly portraits of Jesus imply that the scholars have taught the filmmakers, much as Jesus' disciples taught the people of Palestine. Indeed, filmmakers have been known to employ researchers and advisors to ensure a measure of authenticity in one area or another. Such research efforts are clearly attested in a number of Jesus movies and may be convincing to the general audience. A viewer familiar with early Christian literature and New Testament scholarship may be somewhat skeptical, however. D. W. Griffith's 1916 silent film *Intolerance*, for example, interweaves the so-called Judean story of Jesus with three other narratives from different time periods. Relying on the expertise of advisors such as a Rabbi Isadore Myers, the film explains Jewish groups and customs in a way that at least sounds scholarly, while at the same time conveying Griffith's strong ideological agenda. Hence the Pharisees are described as "a learned Jewish party, the name possibly brought into disrepute by hypocrites among them." This intertitle may have been intended to absolve the Jews as a whole, and the Pharisees as a group, from the charge of hypocrisy, but it did not prevent Griffith from portraying Jesus primarily as a victim of Pharisaic intolerance and hypocrisy. Another note explains, "Wine was deemed a fit offering to God; the drinking of it a part of the Jewish religion." At the same time as it explains the context of the Cana miracle, when Jesus turned water into wine, this note also promotes Griffith's antitemperance agenda, which is prominent elsewhere in the film.

Similarly, the Passion Play in *Jesus of Montreal* claims to draw on historical research. Daniel Coulombe is shown to be receiving precious secrets from a theologian in a parking garage. The theologian's plea that

Daniel not tell anyone evokes the theme of the messianic secret so prominent in Mark's Gospel. But to those viewers who actually know something about first-century Palestine and historical Jesus research, some of the so-called historical facts as presented in the Passion Play are problematic. The Passion Play comments that ancient Jews identified Jesus as the illegitimate son of a Roman soldier, Panthera. It also refers, however, to the discovery of a text containing the name Panthera, implying that this text substantiates the identification of Jesus as Yeshu ben Panthera. To viewers unversed in life of Jesus research, this latter detail might suggest that this identification is an accepted historical fact rather than the anti-Christian polemic of rabbinic literature of some 1500 years ago.[24]

The film that relies most extensively on historical research is Zeffirelli's *Jesus of Nazareth*. By his own admission, Zeffirelli intended this film to be rigorously didactic and gathered scriptural experts to help him to avoid errors and inaccuracies.[25] Nevertheless, Zeffirelli did not want to become a "slave to data," as he put it. A filmmaker has to leave room for the "fruit of the imagination."[26]

Most Jesus films, however, privilege the imagination over historical research. Pasolini, for example, explicitly disavows any interest in exactitude and deliberately did not consult scholars for his *Gospel According to St. Matthew*.[27] He admits to omitting important political and social factors. Such omissions are justified by his purpose, which was not to reconstruct Jesus as he really was but to "reconsecrate" or "remythicize" him.[28] Other films blatantly disregard both scholarship and the Gospel narratives themselves. In contrast to Pasolini's film, which adds virtually no dialogue to the text of Matthew's Gospel, George Stevens's *The Greatest Story Ever Told* has Jesus recite the famous ode to love of 1 Corinthians 13, a passage penned by Paul some years after Jesus' death.

Similarly free, but far more sophisticated, is Scorcese's *Last Temptation of Christ*. This movie explicitly challenges the notion that history, "what really happened," is important to faith. The extended dream sequence experienced by Scorcese's Jesus contains a confrontation between Paul, who preaches Christ crucified and raised from the dead, and Jesus, who has left his wild youth behind and now leads an uneventful domestic existence with Mary, Martha, and their children.

In shock and dismay, Jesus demands that Paul stop preaching that Jesus was crucified and came to life again. To this Paul responds that the only hope for the despairing people around him is the *resurrected* Jesus. "I don't care whether you are Jesus or not," states Paul. "The resurrected Jesus will save the world and that's all that matters. . . . I created the truth out of what people needed and what they believed" (emphasis in original). The irony, of course, is that the extended dream takes place while Jesus is hanging on the cross. Who knows the truth, the dreamer or the apostle?

The drive to portray a Jesus who is more or less Jewish does not necessarily reflect a commitment to the most recent theories in historical Jesus research. A far greater impact can be attributed to a powerful cultural force that has influenced scholars and filmmakers alike, namely, the desire to avoid anti-Semitism in the wake of the Holocaust. Scholar Séan Freyne, for example, argues that "To water down the Jewishness of Galilee and thereby to deny the Jewishness of Jesus not only has the potential for anti-Semitism . . . it also involves a refusal to acknowledge that the Christian understanding of God is grounded in the Jewish experience. . . . In our post-Auschwitz humility, when Christians want to continue to claim the ultimacy of Jesus, it is the ultimacy of the God of Jesus that they are affirming, not another God who supersedes this God of Israel."[29]

The desire to avoid anti-Semitism, or at least to circumvent strong and public Jewish protest, had influenced earlier Jesus films such as *Intolerance.* Following upon strong protests by B'nai Brith, Griffith had removed a large number of segments depicting the Jewish leaders as crucifying Jesus. These changes reduced the Judean story to a mere twelve minutes of this three-and-a-half hour opus.[30] But the efforts to avoid anti-Jewish representation became much more prominent in the post-Holocaust period.[31] Whereas many New Testament scholars assert that both the Jewish authorities and Roman government contributed to the events that culminated in Jesus' crucifixion,[32] some filmmakers emphasize the Roman role so as to avoid any possible charges of anti-Semitism. According to film historian Gerald Forshey, "To choose any interpretation other than one that mitigated the scriptural contention of Jewish culpability was to risk being a bigot."[33]

Zeffirelli, for example, testifies to having been deeply moved by *Nostra Aetate*, the declaration of Vatican II absolving the Jews as a people of collective guilt in the death of Jesus.[34] Zeffirelli's *Jesus of Nazareth* aims not only to portray a Jewish Jesus, as we have already seen, but to evoke the tragedy of blaming the Jews for Jesus' death.[35] A similar impulse is at work in the final scenes of *Jesus of Montreal*, which contrast the crowded halls and inhumane attitude at Montreal's St. Mark's Hospital with the serenity of the Jewish General Hospital and the compassion of its staff people. Contributing to this point is the visual detail of the Star of David on the uniforms of the hospital workers which subtly evokes the badge worn by Jewish residents of the ghettos and concentration camps of the Nazi regime. This scene powerfully asserts that the Christians at St. Mark's have rejected the dying Jesus, whereas the Jews have taken him in. To Montrealers, however, the scene is a source of some humor; it seems that the real Jewish General is not nearly so serene and uncrowded as its portrayal in this scene.

The desire to avoid anti-Semitism creates problems for both scholars and filmmakers in dealing with the Gospel texts that depict conflict between Jesus and the Jews. The way in which this conflict is explained by historians or portrayed on film has important implications for the theme of Jesus' Jewishness. Some scholars narrow the arena of conflict by indicating that Jesus' conflict was not with the Jews as a whole, or even with one entire group of Jews such as the Pharisees, but rather with particular individuals who were in charge of the temple cult.[36] This solution is present in Zeffirelli's *Jesus of Nazareth*, which portrays the Sanhedrin's deliberations about Jesus in great detail. Throughout this depiction it is clear that Jesus has both accusers and supporters within the Sanhedrin, as Nicodemus, a Pharisee himself, informs Jesus. But the Jewish villain of the piece is a fictional character, Zerah the scribe. Zerah functions as the executive director, so to speak, of the Sanhedrin. It is he who manipulates Judas into betraying Jesus and it is he who masterminds the plot to have Jesus executed by the Romans. Blaming Zerah for the death of Jesus allows Zeffirelli to absolve Judas and, to some extent, the Sanhedrin, of primary responsibility.

Many movies soften the Gospels' account of Jesus' conflict with the Jews by simply omitting some of the more difficult scenes and sayings.

For example, *Scorcese's Last Temptation* omits Jesus' appearance before the Jewish authorities. A number of films omit Pilate's washing his hands of responsibility for Jesus' death, and the Jewish outcry, "Let his blood be on us and our children" (Matt 27:25), appears only rarely. The deflection of responsibility to the Romans is criticized strongly by some film reviewers, most notably by Dwight Macdonald, who refers to the Romans of the Jesus films as "fall goys."[37] Although Macdonald strongly refutes accusations of anti-Semitism,[38] he insists that the story of Jesus should be told with reverence for the New Testament text but with irreverence for the sensibilities of contemporary religious groups, including Jews.[39]

Not all post-Holocaust films, however, downplay Jewish responsibility for Jesus' death. *Jesus Christ Superstar* (1993), for example, features black-clad priests and Pharisees standing menacingly on a scaffold in the role of Jesus' primary antagonists.[40] Of the contemporary Jesus films, Pasolini's *Gospel According to St. Matthew* most clearly and unequivocally places the blame for Jesus' death on Jewish shoulders. In contrast to other Jesus movies, Pasolini presents the woes against the Pharisaic hypocrites (Matt 23) in full, including Jesus' sevenfold repetition of the judgment, "Woe to you scribes and Pharisees, hypocrites." Pasolini's personal comments on Jews and the State of Israel are no less disturbing.

> The kibbutzim although they are profoundly sad and recall the concentration camps and the Jews' tendency towards masochism and self-exclusion are at the same time something extremely noble, one of the most democratic and socially advanced experiments I've ever seen. Moreover, I have always loved the Jews because they have been excluded, because they are objects of racial hatred, because they have been forced to be separate from society. But once they've founded their own state they are not different, they're not a minority, they're not excluded: they are the majority, they are the norm. . . . They, who had always been the champions of difference, of martyrdom, of the fight of the other against the normal had now become the majority and the normal and that was something I found . . . a bit hard to swallow.[41]

For a number of filmmakers, including Pasolini, the conflict between Jesus and various groups is intended not as a historical reference, nor as a way of blaming twentieth-century Jews for the death of Jesus. Rather, the conflict is intended to be an analogy to, or perhaps even an allegory of, contemporary conflicts. In Griffith's film, Jesus' struggle against intolerance is paralleled to other stories situated in other places and times. The villains of the so-called modern story, set in the early years of the present century, for example, are portrayed as parallel to the Pharisees of the Jesus story. In *Jesus Christ Superstar*, Judas, played by a black actor, draws a direct analogy between the situation of Jesus and that of racial minorities in the United States subject to a major social and political power. Pasolini's stated goal was to compare the conflict between Jesus and the Jewish authorities in first-century Palestine to religious conflict in twentieth-century Italy.[42] This is not explicit in the film but implied particularly through the appearance and dress of the populace, the Romans, and the Jews.

*Jesus of Montreal* also draws a modern-day analogy, between the ancient Pharisees and the Catholic Church in Quebec. In the Passion Play, Jesus angrily confronts the clerics who have curtailed the successful run of the play by applying the invective of Matthew 23 to the priests and "reverend fathers" of the church. The Pharisees are not mentioned explicitly, though anyone familiar with the Gospel of Matthew will understand the reference.

The effect of such allegory is to remove Jesus even further from the specific Jewish context of first-century Judaism. A similar effect occurs as a result of the need of filmmakers to take into account the variety of theological claims made for Jesus. Historical Jesus researchers often omit discussion of the Gospels' theological claims. Filmmakers, on the other hand, must decide whether or how to portray a divine aspect to Jesus' identity. In *Jesus Christ Superstar*, both Mary Magdalene and Judas emphasize that Jesus "is a man, he's just a man." Scorcese's Jesus, on the other hand, becomes ever more conscious of his divine nature, and in doing so ever more distant from his Jewish identity. He proclaims himself to be God, and then cries out, "God is not an Israelite!"

To conclude, I return to Jesus and his question, "Who do people say that I am?" Historical Jesus research and Jesus movies share the conviction that Jesus' Jewishness is at least part of the answer. To the extent that they consider the social, linguistic, cultural, and religious context of the historical Jesus, scholars and filmmakers alike affirm first-century Judaism, a Semitic language such as Hebrew or Aramaic, and Palestine as central to Jesus' setting and identity. But there are aspects in both scholarship and movies that attenuate this assertion. Those scholars who consider Jesus to have been a Cynic-like sage, a representative of Mediterranean peasant culture, and/or an antinationalist user of metaphorical speech deflect attention from his rootedness in the particularities of first-century Palestinian Judaism, though they do not thereby deny his ethnic Jewish identity. Filmmakers who focus on Jesus as a divine figure, or as the quintessential human being, take his identity far beyond Jewish boundaries and thereby imply that Jesus' Jewishness is not as important to our understanding of him as other factors are.

If such matters were decided by ballot, I would cast mine with Sanders, Freyne, and Fredriksen for an apocalyptic, eschatologically inclined Jesus firmly anchored in the Jewish practices and modes of thought of his time and place. That is my opinion as a New Testament scholar. This view, I suppose, should make me favor Zeffirelli's *Jesus of Nazareth* as the film version that most clearly corresponds to the scholarly portrait of the Jewish Jesus. Yet as a Jew participating willy-nilly in North American popular culture, I hesitate. While I appreciate the sympathetic portrayal of particular Jews including Pharisees and the use of Hebrew liturgical language and familiar-sounding synagogue cadences, I am nevertheless troubled. For all the emphasis on Jewish background and identity, Zeffirelli's *Jesus of Nazareth* ultimately does not escape a supersessionist ideology, particularly in the Last Supper scene. Zeffirelli himself remarked that "the Last Supper was set up according to traditional Jewish ritual and marked the moment when Jesus superseded the ancient rite and gave his disciples and all humanity the Eucharistic mystery."[43]

More congenial, therefore, are those film versions that attenuate the Jewishness of Jesus by drawing an explicit analogy to a contemporary situation. Thus, I am attracted not to Pasolini's *Gospel According to St. Matthew*, in which the analogy is not readily apparent to a North American audience, but to Arcand's *Jesus of Montreal*, in which the critique of the church in Quebec is blatant, and to Scorcese's *Last Temptation of Christ*, which reflects Kazantzakis's focus on the universal struggle between flesh and spirit rather more than it does the Gospels' accounts of the struggle between Jesus and the Pharisees.

The answers to Jesus' vital question, "Who do people say that I am?" are just as varied and complex in our time as those recorded in the synoptic Gospels. As in the biblical passage, one can distinguish between the perceptions of those to whom the Jesus of history is a principal preoccupation—the disciples of Jesus and the scholars of our time—and those to whom he is but one interest among many. But who is right? The Gospel passage favors the disciples, who, through Peter, identify Jesus as the Christ, over those who view Jesus as Elijah, John the Baptist, or one of the prophets. But although the disciples have supplied the correct title, their understanding of its meaning and implications is incomplete. Only a few verses after Peter's glorious declaration, Jesus chastises him in the strongest terms for not understanding and accepting the necessity of Jesus' death and the promise of resurrection (Mark 8:33). Later the disciples bicker like small children over who is to sit next to Jesus at the table of his glory (Mark 10:37).

We scholars might take these examples as a warning that our own understanding may also be incomplete. If we do not all go so far as to admit, with Martin Scorcese, that Jesus can be reinvented to suit anyone's needs,[44] we may at least acknowledge that a variety of contemporary concerns and personal viewpoints will determine whether we see Jesus as man, as God, as Jew, as peasant, as symbol of human struggle, or as the savior of humankind.

NOTES

1. Parallels are found in Matt 16:13–15 and Luke 9:18–20.

2. See Roy Kinnard and Tim Davis, *Divine Images: A History of Jesus on the Screen* (New York: Citadel Press, 1992); Lloyd Baugh, *Imaging the Divine: Jesus and Christ-Figures in Film* (Kansas City, Mo.: Sheed & Ward, 1997); W. Barnes Tatum, *Jesus at the Movies* (Santa Rosa, Calif.: Polebridge Press, 1997); Peter T. Chattaway, "Jesus in the Movies," *Bible Review* (February 1998): 28–35, 45–46;

Gerald E. Forshey, "The Jesus Cycle," in *American Religious and Biblical Spectaculars* (Westport, Conn.: Praeger, 1992), 83–121.

3. William Klassen, "The Mediterranean Jesus: Context," in *Whose Historical Jesus?* ed. William E. Arnal and Michel Desjardins (Waterloo, Ont.: Wilfrid Laurier University Press, 1997), 6. The documentary *From Jesus to Christ* emphasizes and explores Jesus' Jewish identity in detail.

4. See E. P. Sanders, *Jesus and Judaism* (London: SCM Press, 1985); E. P. Sanders, *The Historical Figure of Jesus* (London: Penguin Books, 1993); Geza Vermes, *Jesus and the World of Judaism* (London: SCM Press, 1983); Séan Freyne, *Galilee, Jesus, and the Gospels: Literary Approaches and Historical Investigations* (Philadelphia: Fortress Press, 1988); Paula Fredriksen, "What You See Is What You Get: Context and Content in Current Research on the Historical Jesus," *Theology Today* 52 (April 1995): 75–97.

5. E. P. Sanders, "Jesus and the First Table of the Jewish Law," in *Jews and Christians Speak of Jesus*, ed. Arthur E. Zannoni (Minneapolis: Fortress Press, 1994), 71.

6 . William E. Arnal, "Making and Re-Making the Jesus-Sign: Contemporary Markings on the Body of Christ," in Arnal and Desjardins, *Whose Historical Jesus?* 310.

7. Lawrence H. Schiffman, "The Jewishness of Jesus: Commandments Concerning Interpersonal Relations," in Zannoni, *Jews and Christians*, 39.

8. Sanders, *Historical Figure of Jesus*, 254–64.

9. Tatum, *Jesus at the Movies*, 145.

10. Franco Zeffirelli, *Zeffirelli's Jesus: A Spiritual Diary*, trans. Willis J. Egan, S.J. (San Francisco: Harper & Row, 1984 [Italian original, 1977]), 45.

11. Ibid., 59.

12. Ibid., 68.

13. Fredriksen, "What You See," 80.

14. John Dominic Crossan, *The Historical Jesus: The Life of a Mediterranean Jewish Peasant* (San Francisco: HarperSanFrancisco, 1991), 263.

15. Fredriksen, "What You See," 81–82.

16. Arnal, "Making and Re-Making," 310.

17. Tatum, *Jesus at the Movies*, 164–65.

18. It must be said that no cinematic Jesus would make the best groomed (let alone the best dressed) list, except perhaps for Max von Sydow in George Stevens's *The Greatest Story Ever Told*.

19. See Marcus J. Borg, *Jesus in Contemporary Scholarship* (Valley Forge, Pa.: Trinity Press International, 1994); N. T. Wright, *The New Testament and the People of God* (Minneapolis: Fortress Press, 1992); N. T. Wright, *Jesus and the Victory of God* (Minneapolis: Fortress Press, 1996).

20. Fredriksen, "What You See," 86.

21. Wright, *Jesus and the Victory*, 228.

22 . Borg, *Jesus in Contemporary Scholarship*, 26.

23 . Fredriksen, "What You See," 88.

24. On the portrayal of Jesus in rabbinic literature, see Jacob Z. Lauterbach, "Jesus in the Talmud," in *Jewish Expressions on Jesus: An Anthology*, ed. Trude Weiss-Rosmarin (New York: KTAV, 1976), 1–98 (originally published in Jacob Z. Lauterbach, *Rabbinic Essays* [New York: KTAV, 1973], 473–570).

25. Zeffirelli, *Zeffirelli's Jesus*, 39.

26. Ibid., 37.

27. Oswald Stack, *Pasolini on Pasolini: Interviews with Oswald Stack* (Bloomington, Ind.: Indiana University Press, 1970), 82.

28. Ibid., 83.

29. Séan Freyne, "Galilean Questions to Crossan's Mediterranean Jesus," in Arnal and Desjardins, *Whose Historical Jesus?* 91.

30. Chattaway, "Jesus in the Movies," 31.

31. Forshey, "Jesus Cycle," 83.

32. See, for example, Sanders, *Historical Figure of Jesus*, 265–75.

33. Forshey, "Jesus Cycle," 93.

34. Zeffirelli, *Zeffirelli's Jesus*, 6.

35. Ibid., 11.

36. Fredriksen, "What You See," 96.

37. Dwight Macdonald, *Dwight Macdonald on the Movies* (New York: Prentice-Hall, 1969), 428, 436.

38. Ibid., 429

39. Ibid., 431.

40. In her review of the film for *Christianity Today* (12 October 1973), Cheryl Forbes commented that although the film is a theological disaster, it is an ecumenical triumph because all groups condemned it. See Tatum, *Jesus at the Movies*, 129.

41. Stack, *Pasolini on Pasolini*, 76.

42. Tatum, *Jesus at the Movies*, 112.

43. Zeffirelli, *Zeffirelli's Jesus*, 101.

44. Quoted in Chattaway, "Jesus in the Movies," 45.

# 8. JESUS IN THE EYES OF ONE JEWISH SCHOLAR

*Alan F. Segal*

In the eighteenth and nineteenth centuries, the truth of the Gospel stories was brought into doubt by the philosophies of the Enlightenment. What makes the stories of the Old or New Testament any more historically probable than Aesop's fables or Grimm's fairy tales? Their truth depends entirely on one source (or it did then and it pretty much still does, though we have some archaeological finds that previous scholars did not have) whose authority is entirely due to religious predisposition and not to rational principles.

As a way of combating this cultured critique of religion, a number of scholars throughout the nineteenth and twentieth centuries developed criteria that would apply to any historical source, such as the New Testament, which was written from the perspective of people who had already accepted the truth of its major propositions. A number of important criteria were adduced—Jewish background, multiple and early attestation, embarrassment—but they were all made subordinate to what most people call "the criterion of dissimilarity" (including embarrassment, of course), which is without doubt the most important of all criteria with regard to the historiographical question and to the issue of the historicity of Jesus.[1] This is what it says in plain English: To arrive at an undoubted fact in the life of Jesus, one must eliminate everything that is in the interest of the Church to tell; or, conversely, for a fact or saying to be held historical, it must not be in the interest of the Church to tell it. To use other similar language, it must be an embarrassment for the early Church.

This is a very hard test. By any rational appraisal, many things Jesus actually said or did will be eliminated by this criterion. Furthermore, and this is where it most binds on me, it completely negates the issue of Jesus' Jewish background, because anything Jesus said or did that was also said or done in early Judaism is suspect: dissimilarity usually implies dissimilarity with the Jewish environment as well. Why then use it?

It was designed not to write a biography of Jesus but to answer the challenge of the cultured despiser of Christianity as to whether anything is historical in the Gospels. It also has developed the secondary and very important function, if I may be allowed an outside observation, of cautioning persons of different interpretations in Christianity from getting overconfident about their own confessions.

So what passes this very hard criterion? Does anything? The answer is "Yes!" Did Jesus really live? The answer is "Yes!" And, of course, this is the most important part of using it, for if some things pass then we know that Jesus existed: Jesus was baptized by John, he preached the end of the world, he opposed the temple, and he was crucified. (No one actually saw him rise.) Gone are the Davidic ancestry, the birth stories, many if not most of his sayings, and his healings. Clearly we are not saying that these events did not happen. We are just saying we cannot be one hundred percent sure that they happened, so they cannot be used as evidence for the existence of Jesus. This sum total of scandal about Jesus, the modern historical scandal of the cross, is not enough to build a biography. But, of course, one forgets the original purpose of these arguments—to demonstrate that Jesus was an historical character, even if we know little about him.

Many Jews understand the import of the challenge and would be very surprised to hear a Jewish scholar say that the existence of Jesus has been proved beyond a rational doubt. But I think we have to give the criterion its due: it has served its purpose in answering the question. By the use of the criterion, we can be as sure as we are of anything in history. That is, of course, a very different thing from saying that he was resurrected or that the tomb is empty. But to say he lived is to say that the cultured despiser of Christianity is answered: the New Testament is not Grimm's fairy fales. (On the other hand, it is not the *Congressional Record* either.)

Many important and well-trained New Testament scholars leave the issue there. Why get onto unsure ground, and why risk entering into discourse that is bound to start interdenominational polemics? Indeed, there are many historical issues, especially in the ancient period, that we cannot verify exactly. There are probably more of the unprovable kinds of incidents than the ones of which we can be sure. So Jesus' existence is already one of the more certain, verifiable, and assured answers that we have when it comes to the brute facts of history.

But ending the matter with the few facts that pass the criterion is not the only possible place to stop. For one thing, it is almost always a dissatisfying place to be. For Christians it is very dissatisfying, because they are left with a mysterious Jesus with few if any teachings or healings and who stands against a black background, a constant cipher. Even for non-Christian scholars it is very frustrating, as I already mentioned, because it prevents us from saying very much about Jesus' Judaism. I always want to go beyond these hard and important criteria because virtually everything about Jesus' Jewish background has been eliminated by the criterion of dissimilarity.

But beware anyone who goes beyond this, because we leave the area of securely known facts and enter an area where we know much less, have less confidence, and, what is more, where the value of our arguments is far more relative that what we just discussed. We enter into an area where we must be satisfied with less than surety. And we enter an area where, consciously or not, everyone will want to validate his or her personal or denominational faith. For people whose very faith depends on the reality of Jesus in their lives, this can be very confusing. How can one be sure of his existence and continued presence in one's life on one side and be skeptical of his biography on the other? It is a hard stance. But that is the peculiar problem of the person of faith who wants to play in a world of modern historiography.

We must be prepared to say we have no complete proofs or demonstrations. We must be satisfied with inferences and degrees of surety much less than we would like. And, most important, we are not free to ignore conclusions from the previous studies, because they remain just as true in any discussions of the likely life of Jesus. In sum, to enter into the whole discussion of what Jesus was like is to enter into a very unsure and unsettling discussion.

So how would I place Jesus within his Jewish environment? How do I come up with a consistent story by connecting some dots? I think one must begin with several assured or virtually assured conclusions. Jesus lived and died as a Jew for his Judaism, some of which was possibly subversive to the powers of his day and some of which impressed Rome as politically dangerous. He was the leading figure in a small movement of Jews who saw his death as a martyrdom, like many previous Jewish martyrdoms. It was evidently his earliest disciples who saw a victory in the Easter event, the empty tomb (though possibly that is a later addition to the story since Paul does not mention it), and interpreted it as a sign that Jesus had been resurrected from the dead and ascended to heaven to sit next to God. I feel sure that the earliest Christians experienced the continued presence of Jesus in their lives, not in some attenuated form but in the form of resurrected Messiah, angel of the Lord, Son of man (all at once), who was enthroned next to God. (This seems clearly true and does not really come into the criterion of dissimilarity at all, because it is simply what the Church states as its belief.) Paul identified Jesus as risen savior and messiah on account of his ecstatic experience—but not apparently the "Son of man" in Daniel, or at least he is silent about that particular identification.

The Gospels show that the Son of man identification is early and important; they proclaim that the man Jesus as resurrected became the figure prophesied in Dan 7:13, a figure the church calls the "Son of man," but that is probably better understood as a reference to "a man-like figure in heaven" and not a title at all. We know how they made this identification, that it was part of the kerygma of the early Church, and that it was consistent with Paul's ecstatic and visionary Christianity.

Clearly, the Gospels make this identification on the basis of two other Hebrew Bible quotations—Psalm 110 and Psalm 8. The three passages together can almost be read as a narrative of the resurrection and ascension of Jesus as the figure enthroned next to God. We do not know why the Gospels make this identification except that the figure was part of a very famous apocalyptic document, the visions of Dan 7–13, which is the first place where resurrection is mentioned unambiguously in the Hebrew Bible, and where it is promised to martyrs.

Whether we can take this fact back a few years and posit that Daniel
figured prominently in Jesus' teaching (I think it must have) or not is difficult to tell, just as it is difficult to tell today, when a known figure is quoted
by a newspaper, what exactly that person said. But we know it is an early
and strong tradition and it is impossible to explain without an apocalyptic (not just eschatological) content in Jesus' preaching. Jesus must
have preached repentance for the coming end of the world and recommended a radical change of behavior as the only way to cope with these
events. He was, in the words of my colleagues Marcus Borg and John
Dominic Crossan, an eschatological Jesus; but I think he was even
more—an apocalypticist—which will mark me as different from both
Borg's Jesus and several of the others. By this I mean he was a millen-
nialist prophet of a movement like those religious movements we can
see among oppressed groups everywhere. A traditional worldview is
being deeply challenged by a different religious system, just as its economic and social life is being challenged by superior force and desire to
exploit and expropriate. These are always movements with political
implications, but the language is almost always determinedly religious.
More often than not, the movement's political and religious aims are
easily disconfirmed, but sometimes only the political past is lost and the
group survives religiously. Christianity is one of these rare movements
in world history. The reasons for its survival are unique, independent,
and subtle. But they can be outlined. Here is my version of the story:

Although Christianity's destiny brought it to Rome and world
prominence, its beginnings were in "sectarian" Judaism. The Church
taught the death and resurrection of Jesus, but Jesus' own message is
harder to isolate. Jesus may have taught many things. He seems to have
been a teacher of wisdom and ethics, but the apocalyptic part of the
early message of Christianity must have been part of his teachings.
Indeed, the Jesus movement resembles several other apocalyptic movements in first-century Judaism.

Until recently, apocalypticism was defined solely by the literary
apocalypses, especially the book of Daniel in the Hebrew Bible and the
Revelation of St. John in the New Testament. Apocalypticism, coming
from the Greek verb meaning to "disclose," "uncover," or "bring to

light," has always implied the revelation of the secret of the coming end-time. Apocalyptic books have in common the violent end of the world and the establishment of God's kingdom. They are replete with arcane symbolism and puzzling visions, the meaning of which is hardly clear from a first reading. And they are often pseudepigraphal, fictitiously ascribed to an earlier hero or patriarch.

The discovery of the Dead Sea Scrolls and the subsequent renewed interest in many apocryphal and pseudepigraphal books of the Old and New Testaments has changed our understanding of apocalypticism by providing insight into the conditions that produced the literary genre. The Dead Sea Scrolls make accessible for the first time the daily workings of an actual apocalyptic community, comparing their social organization with their apocalyptic writings.

Jesus spoke of the "Son of man" and the resurrection of the dead, both apocalyptic prophecies found in the book of Daniel. Before the fateful events of Jesus' Passover pilgrimage to Jerusalem, these notions could hardly have been fully distinguished from more political expectations of the coming of God's kingdom, with the possible help of the Messiah. Although early Christianity was a religious revolution, its political aims were yet inchoate. Some of Jesus' followers seem to have had revolutionary expectations, though passive revolution (maintaining ethical and cultic purity so that God and his angels could bring about political change) was the stronger tradition in Judaism, as the Qumran community shows us.

Although Jesus recommended passive resistance—he did not resist when arrested, for instance—he was still an apocalypticist who had strong feelings of scorn for the putative rulers of his country. The message of Jesus, that with repentance all are equal before God, is typical of all sectarian apocalypticism of the time. Christian practices of public repentance, baptism, and chaste communal living are likewise typical of other contemporary apocalyptic groups.

Yet the similarity only emphasizes the striking difference between Christianity and the Dead Sea Scrolls. The Jesus movement equated the purity laws with moral laws, just as the Dead Sea Scroll movement did. But the Jesus movement was not priestly in orientation; rather, it gave special attention to redeeming sinners who had violated the purity rules. Its corresponding emphasis on converting the distressed or sinful began in the teaching of John the Baptist, became characteristically Christian, and probably reflected the strong charismatic influence of Jesus. But it was not totally uninterested in purity either, as the rite of the baptism itself shows. Through John the Baptist, baptism became the Christian rite uniquely demonstrating repentance, though there is no good evidence that Jesus performed it.

Although Jesus accepted the Jewish law, he occasionally indulged in symbolic actions designed to provoke questions about the purpose of the Torah, such as healing the chronically ill or picking grain on the Sabbath. But these actions could have been directed at the Pharisees or other sectarian interpreters of the Torah without implying that the Torah itself was invalid.

As the Christian movement developed, some Christians showed signs of a primitive communalism, implicit in their pooling of resources. Christianity did not adhere to the social code of the Essenes, yet it did contain the seeds of a radical criticism of private property and believed strongly in sharing all economic resources. "No man can serve two masters. . . . You cannot serve God and mammon [money]" (Luke 16:13).

Jesus was suspicious of people of means: "It is easier for a camel to go through the eye of a needle than for a rich man to enter the kingdom of God" (Mark 10:24). This statement does not prevent a rich man from becoming part of the movement, but it establishes a higher price for the rich than the poor. Given the command to share all things with the poor, few confident and successful people would have entered the movement at first. Those whose wealth had brought with it feelings of achievement or worth would have been better targets for evangelism. However, the overturning of the tables of the moneylenders in the temple at Passover, a time of heightened worries over mob actions, brought him to the attention of the authorities. Crucifixion is a method of execution that the Romans used for political offenders, among other things, to set an example of the consequences of rebellion.

In the Gospel of Mark, Jesus denies the title "Messiah" whenever it is applied to him (see 8:27–31, for instance) except at the trial. But someone must have had messianic expectations of him, because that is the charge listed on the cross: "King of the Jews." The crucifixion extinguished any political messianic expectations, but it was the very title that his followers felt had been vindicated by the experience of resurrection. Though the Gospels are clear that no one actually saw the event, his followers became convinced of the reality of the resurrection, which is exactly the reward that apocalyptic works promise for martyrs. Furthermore, since the resurrection had already happened, the end of time must also already be upon us. From this point onward, Christians have believed that we are living in the end of days, which will see fulfilled the kingdom of God. Jesus' resurrected body of glory appeared several times to Paul, showing him that those who believe in the risen Christ will soon follow him into the kingdom in a transformed, even angelic, state. All of these beliefs are understandable as Jewish apocalyptic beliefs transformed by the events of the fateful Easter in which Jesus journeyed to Jerusalem to worship his God.

## NOTES

1. See John Gager, *Kingdom and Community: The Social World of Early Christianity* (Englewood Cliffs, N. J.: Prentice-Hall, 1975), especially 2–18. An earlier and more elaborate form of this argument may be found in my "Jesus and First-Century Judaism," in *Jesus at 2000*, ed. Marcus Borg (Boulder, Colo.: Westview, 1997), 55–72.

# 9. JESUS AS OTHER PEOPLE'S SCRIPTURE

*Jonathan D. Brumberg-Kraus*

In his study of Paul, the Jewish scholar Alan Segal remarked that "all [of a considerable number of Jewish scholars on Paul] tell us more about the predicament of Jewish existence in the twentieth century than they tell us about Paul."[1] Does that mean that Jewish study of Jesus tells us primarily about the Jewish scholars themselves, and not much about Jesus? My own work on the topic has been criticized for suggesting that there is nothing else but Jewish ideology in the Jewish study of Christian origins.[2] I am sure the same kinds of objections were considered at the symposium. However, it is my contention in this essay that contemporary Jewish critical scholarship has something very significant to say about the nature of what Christians call Jesus Christ, beyond what it says about the scholars themselves. Contemporary Jewish scholarship reflects a new understanding of Jesus, one that requires neither the insistence on his humanity or the denial of his divinity, but rather recognizes him as *other people's* (i.e., Christians') religious concept or symbol. Jewish scholarship on Jesus is the expression of a pluralistic cultural context that acknowledges what may be sacred to one religious community may not be to another. We recognize and study the Jesus Christ who is sacred and religiously meaningful to Christians, but not to us, or at least, not in the same way.

Jewish scholarship on Jesus accentuates two points: the importance of context for understanding interpretations of Jesus and the relational character of who Jesus is. The importance of context for understanding the meaning of symbols is aptly illustrated by Clifford Geertz's analogy in his classic essay on "Ideology as a Cultural System." What does it mean to praise a pretty girl as the "cream in my coffee" in a society that

155

drinks its coffee black?[3] That is what it was like when some American Reform Jewish scholars stressed the Jewishness of Jesus in the face of insistent Christian missionizing and Jewish assimilationism toward the end of the nineteenth century. But it meant something quite different when Joseph Klausner wrote on the Jewishness of Jesus in modern Hebrew to an audience of Jewish intellectuals engaged in the building of a Jewish state in the 1920s.[4] And yet it is still another thing when post-Holocaust era liberal Jewish intellectuals stress the importance of studying Christian origins to a dual audience of American Jews anxious about their Jewish identity and continuity, and of Christian and secular academics with whom they seek to cultivate collegial relations. Now that disputations and pogroms are passé, today's more secular, pluralistic climate has heightened the opportunities and dangers of social exchange.[5] Jewish study of Jesus in this context is like praising him as the "cream in my coffee" to a mixed society of black coffee drinkers, those who like it with cream, and those who prefer tea. The importance of the sociohistorical context of Jesus studies underlines the second point, the relational character of Jesus. As for Jews, so for the broader culture; who Jesus is depends on who is talking to whom and when. So does that mean that interpretations of Jesus are all subjective and relative? No. *Relational* is not the same thing as *relative*. To say that Jesus' character is relational and must be understood contextually means rather that we have to be precise about the context and the relationships behind the question of Jesus: "Who do people say that I am?"

From my place as a twentieth-century Jewish scholar of comparative religion and a Reconstructionist rabbi, I say Jesus is "other people's scripture." This is a general category of religious phemonena that accurately and precisely reflects the way that our contemporary society, where Jews critically study Jesus, relates to Jesus.[6] By defining Jesus as "other people's scripture," I mean to emphasize these four aspects of his character:

- Jesus is something sacred to people other than the interpreters (Jesus is *other people's* scripture)

- Jesus is not (just) an experience or a personality, but embodied as a "text"

- Jesus functions as a revered text in a specific religious system (Jesus is other people's *scripture*)

- As such, Jesus is a "relational concept"[7] (Jesus is *both* "other people's" and "scripture")

Contemporary Jewish scholars like those who participated in the Klutznick Symposium tend to emphasize or reflect these approaches to Jesus. Our complex relationship to Jesus exemplifies the complex function Jesus plays in broader contemporary culture.

In the most recent trend of American Jewish scholarship on Jesus, Jesus is obviously not the object of primary religious devotion, but his sanctity to *others* as Jesus Christ is understood. This is in contrast to earlier trends in twentieth-century Jewish scholarship, especially outside the United States, that emphasized the Jewish Jesus of history over the Christian Christ of faith. For example, Geza Vermes, in his book *Jesus the Jew: A Historian's Reading of the Gospels*, explained:

> By contrast to the imperatives of faith, the issues which writer and reader will explore together are the primitive, genuine historical significance of words and events recorded in the Gospels.... [T]he present historical investigation ... is prompted by a single-minded and devout search for fact and reality.[8]

Klausner, too, represented this perspective on the Jewishness of the historical Jesus.[9] To be sure, they both reflected the interest in "the historical Jesus" then current among their Christian critical scholarly counterparts. However, since both implied that as Jewish scholars they were more objective than Christian scholars, their emphases were more than just a reflection of their Christian colleagues' agenda.[10] They viewed faith in general, and Christian faith in particular, as serious hindrances to "objective" study of Jesus.[11]

More recent Jewish scholarship embraces critical approaches that treat Christian interpretations of the religious meaning of Jesus as worthy objects of study, not just the historical personality of Jesus. Indeed, recent Jewish studies seem to be focused much more on the religious interpretations of Jesus imbedded in early Christian texts, rather than on the extratextual Jesus of history, which earlier scholars alleged to be behind these later faith-inspired "accretions." Now we have Jewish scholars devoting studies to the development of New Testament Christology (Paula Fredrikson), Pauline interpretations of Christ (Samuel Sandmel, Nancy Fuchs-Kreimer, and Alan Segal), and redaction-critical or literary studies of perspectives on Jesus in the Gospels (Michael Cook on Mark, Amy-Jill Levine on Matthew, Adele Reinhartz on John, myself on Luke,).[12] Again, as with earlier Jewish scholarship, this to some extent reflects broader trends among Christian critical study of the New Testament. Without doing an exhaustive analysis of these trends here, suffice it to say that there is an increasing recognition that the early Christians interpreted the extratextual *event* of the revelation of Jesus in his ministry, death, and resurrection from the same hermeneutical stances that they and other Jewish contemporaries interpreted the *text* of the Bible.[13] In an influential study of early Christian prophecy, M. Eugene Boring, a Christian scholar, states this position succinctly:

> [E]arly Christian prophets functioned as interpreters of scripture in light of contemporary events and as interpreters of events in the light of scripture. Scripture and event go together. *The pairing of revelation-by-word and revelation-by-event is the unmistakable structural analogy* that binds together the theology of the old covenant and its documents, on which early Christianity was founded, and the new eschatological covenant, of which the early Christian prophets understood themselves to be ministers. We separate scripture and event only for the purposes of clarity in discussion, with the understanding that each is understood only in the light of the others.[14]

Paul, the Evangelists, and the composers of hypothetical sources like Q, the new foci of Jewish study, are essentially Christian prophets who treat verses from the Bible, the events of Jesus' life and/or death and resurrection, and his words equivalently as revelations of God—as scripture. Recent Jewish studies of Jesus embrace those current critical approaches that emphasize the transformation of the person and event of Jesus into texts. Since we are talking about a specific kind of text, scripture, which has religious authority for those who recognize it as such, this Jewish scholarship suggests a surprising conclusion about its (our) implicit assumptions. Jewish scholars, too, attribute a certain kind of religious authority to Jesus, albeit indirectly and with qualifications that I am about to discuss. By granting the religious authority Jesus has for the early Christian texts we study (in contrast to the earlier Jewish and secularized Christian scholars who viewed such faith as a hindrance to objective study), we tacitly accept it ourselves—at the very least as a real power in our culture to be reckoned with.

In what forms does my rather bold assertion that Jewish scholars grant some degree of religious authority to Jesus occur? First, let me underline, our acceptance is tacit, indirect, and highly qualified. That is what distinguishes Jewish critical scholars of Jesus from "Jews for Jesus," among other things. One of the most important hints of the indirect way Jewish scholars respect Jesus' religious authority is their frequent use of analogies equating Jesus to religious symbols central to Judaism. Probably the most useful and common analogy is "Jesus Christ is to Christianity what Torah is to Judaism." An example of this analogy is implied in the more complex formulation of a comparative study of the formative categories of Judaism and Christianity coauthored by the Jewish scholar Jacob Neusner and the Christian Bruce D. Chilton: "God, Torah, Israel for Judaism; God, *Christ*, Church for Christianity."[15] Another variation of the analogy is "Christology is to Christianity as *halakhah* is to Judaism," a position advocated by David Novak.[16] I have made the analogy, "the Last Supper is for Christians what the Passover *seder* is for Jews."[17] The effect of these and similar analogies is that Jesus is as religiously significant to Christians as the central symbols of Judaism are religiously significant to Jews.[18] At the very least, these analogies concede that Jesus is religiously significant, as "other people's Torah." Beyond that, they accept his authority as a well-known, dominant cultural symbol shaping the categories of the comparison.

At the same time, emphatic assertions of difference nearly always qualify such analogies. In an earlier formulation, Neusner characterized the relationship between Judaism and Christianity as "different people talking about different things to different people."[19] A Christian

observer of modern Jewish studies of Jesus described them as a "reclamation of Jesus," underlining the point that while Jesus may have originally been "ours," he certainly has belonged to others (i.e., Christians)
over the past two thousand years.[20] Because he has not been ours for so
long, we supposedly have to "*re*-claim" him.

Moreover, when Jewish scholars make Jesus "ours," we are likely to
do so for our own needs as members of the Jewish community—
explicitly or implicitly. In that sense, our recognition of Jesus' power is
not the same as Christians' (or so-called Jews for Jesus). Our motiva-
tions to interpret Jesus are not solely to further Christians' understanding of their central religious symbol, unless that too serves us in our
situation as Jews in America. Precisely because of this, some of my
Jewish colleagues who insist their work is for the broader good have
questioned the wisdom of calling attention to the self-serving aspects of
the Jewish study of Jesus, to how it is "good for the Jews." Yet it is unde-
niable that Jewish critical scholarship on Jesus has served the communal needs of Jews, especially here in America.

In my previous study, I pointed out three ways in which Jewish
scholars have appropriated Jesus and the study of Christian origins to
serve Jewish communal interests. Jewish scholars have studied Jesus to
defend Jews from proselytization or anti-Semitic hostility legitimated
by appeals to Jesus' authority.[21] While this was particularly the position
of Reform Jewish critical scholars in Germany and America from the
mid-nineteenth to the early twentieth century, Samuel Sandmel's more
recent book, *Anti-Semitism in the New Testament?* generally accepted as
the definitive statement of the issue, stands in this tradition.[22] The
agenda behind this approach was to break down the barriers to acculturation to non-Jewish society. Jewish scholars emphasized the
Jewishness of Jesus as an antidote to Christian anti-Semitism. By
appealing to Jesus' authority, their scholarship was in effect arguing,
"We're not as other as you think, since your founder was *fun unzer* [one
of ours]." Jewish scholars also turned their critical attention to Jesus
and early Christianity to subvert Christian cultural dominance. One
way of doing this was to assert Jewish expertise in rabbinic sources, in
the *Jewish* background of Jesus, as the sine qua non of objective critical

scholarship on Jesus.[23] This approach is a critical expression of the Jewish folk belief that "they got everything from us."

Another way to subvert dominant Christian social norms has been for Jewish scholars to stress explicitly that they were studying Jesus and/or other early Christian sources in order to reconstruct Jewish history or to explain Jewish religious concerns, rather than Christian ones. For example, in his seminal study of the Pharisees, Neusner asserted that he was analyzing early Christian traditions about Jesus in order to reconstruct the history and practices of the Jewish Pharisees, not for what they said about early Christian doctrines.[24] In effect, this approach implies that Christian history is background to Jewish history, not the other way around.

Finally, Jewish academic success in the quintessentially Christian fields of Jesus and early Christian studies is the sign of "making it" both in the Jewish and the non-Jewish worlds.[25] Jewish experts in the academic study of Christianity exemplify two typical modern Jewish strategies of acculturation identified by Benjamin Harshav: learning and self-realization.[26] By learning "new languages, 'secular' (i.e., Christian) culture, and rational science," Jewish scholars achieve acceptance in the broader culture. Likewise, Jewish scholarship on the New Testament is a form of self-realization, "not relying any more on traditional structures, but 'doing it' or 'making it' by yourself."[27] Hence, you will often find Jewish scholars of Jesus and Christian origins calling attention to the fact that they are mavericks, that they are "going against the grain" of what their fellow Jews and Christian academics would deem as normal.[28] Sarah Tanzer once aptly characterized the situation of a Jew teaching the New Testament as "double jeopardy."[29] Modern Jewish scholars of the New Testament have appropriated the powerful Christian cultural symbol of Jesus to advance themselves in the two civilizations we live in and value: our Jewish communities and the broader Christian, or secularized Christian society.

One appropriates something only if one values it. We Jewish scholars tacitly acknowledge the authority of Jesus in secularized Christian culture because we want a piece of it, or we do not see ourselves as alienated from it. We insist on Jesus' otherness and our distinctly Jewish approach to him because sometimes it serves our needs to differentiate ourselves as liberals or traditionalists within the Jewish community, and because it reflects our ideal of a pluralistic (not just religiously tolerant) democratic society.[30] However, no matter how self-serving Jewish study of Jesus might be, as a modern process of relating to Jesus, it has something instructive to say to Christians about Jesus. Indeed, it is a significant characteristic of Jesus in modern culture that reverberations of his religious impact can be felt even in the thought of non-Christians.

Jewish scholarship of Jesus is part of a process of the secularization of Jesus' religious significance. This can be stated in three theses:

- Jesus is increasingly objectified as a cultural artifact, a text to be interpreted or otherwise related to, but not an intangible experience accessible only to the chosen few.[31]

- Jesus has an authority in our culture that is not strictly speaking religious, or better, is not religious in an exclusively Christian way.

- We live in a pluralistic culture where to affirm Christ no longer (theo)logically implies "the Jews be damned."[32]

Jewish scholarship of Jesus implies that the affirmation of Christ's divinity and authority no longer need be an either/or proposition, condemning those who deny one or the other to eternal damnation. Rather, in our contemporary culture, Jesus Christ has a primary and secondary authority (as analogous somewhat to Graham's primary and secondary scriptures[33]). His authority is primary to Christians, who accept his divinity, and/or who have experienced his immediate presence. It is secondary to non-Christians who recognize Jesus' power as a cultural symbol in the society in which they live, and who respect the other kinds of power they observe Christ having for and on others. However, they have neither directly experienced him, nor desire to, themselves.

Finally, it is clear that any Christology from now on has to be relational, contextualized in the communities and different historical circumstances in which any sort of "Christ-talk" takes place. Catholic theologian Edward Schillebeeckx has argued this point quite persuasively in his masterful theological-historical study on Jesus.[34] Jewish scholarship on Jesus, which indeed has been a significant influence on contemporary Christian theologians (e.g., Paul van Buren and Elisabeth Schüssler Fiorenza), only reflects the complicated society whose relationship to Jesus must be explicated for an accurate contemporary Christology.[35] The notion that "Jesus is other people's scripture" is my modest effort as a Jew to characterize the relational Christology for today's complex society.

NOTES

1. Alan Segal, *Paul the Convert: The Apostolate and Apostasy of Saul the Pharisee* (New Haven, Conn.: Yale University Press, 1990), 307, note 8.

2. Jonathan Brumberg-Kraus, "A Jewish Ideological Perspective on the Study of Christian Scripture," *Jewish Social Studies* 4:1 (NS): 121–52. I began to respond to this criticism on pages 140–41. This essay extends my response.

3. Clifford Geertz, "Ideology as a Cultural System," *The Interpretation of Cultures* (New York: Basic Books, 1973), 212.

4. Brumberg-Kraus, "Jewish Ideological Perspective," 124.

5. This is the situation of the liberal Jewish intellectual perspectives (my own included) I discuss in Brumberg-Kraus, "Jewish Ideological Perspective," 135–40.

6. See William A. Graham, "Scripture," in *The Encyclopedia of Religion*, ed. Mircea Eliade (New York: Macmillan, 1995), 13:133–45 for the comparative religious theory of scripture upon which my theses are based.

7. The term is Graham's ("Scripture," 134), the application mine.

8. Geza Vermes, *Jesus the Jew: A Historian's Reading of the Gospels* (Philadelphia: Fortress Press, 1973), 16, 17.

9. Brumberg-Kraus, "Jewish Ideological Perspective," 148. David Sandmel, Samuel Sandmel's son, is completing a dissertation on Joseph Klausner that promises to add much to our knowledge about the influence of the Eastern European and Israeli Zionist historical contexts on his view on Jesus.

10. Ibid., 132.

11. See, e.g., Vermes, *Jesus the Jew*, 17: "If after working his [sic] way through this book, the reader recognizes that this man, *so distorted by Christian and Jewish myth alike, was in fact neither the Christ of the Church nor the bogey-man of Jewish popular tradition*, some small beginning may have been made in repayment to him of a debt long overdue [emphasis mine]."

12. Paula Fredriksen, *From Jesus to Christ: The Origins of the New Testament Images of Jesus* (New Haven, Conn.: Yale University Press, 1988); Samuel

Sandmel, *The Genius of Paul: A Study in History* (Philadelphia: Fortress Press, 1979); Nancy Fuchs-Kreimer, "What Scholars Are Saying about Paul: What It Means for Jews," *The Reconstructionist* 51 (March 1986): 11–15, based on her Ph.D. dissertation, "The 'Essential Heresy': Paul's View of the Law According to Jewish Writers, 1886–1986," Temple University (Ann Arbor, Mich.: UMI, 1991); Segal, *Paul the Convert*; Amy-Jill Levine, *The Social and Ethnic Dimensions of Matthean Salvation History*, Studies in the Bible and Early Christianity 14 (Lewiston, N.Y. : Edwin Mellen Press, 1988); Michael J. Cook, *Mark's Treatment of the Jewish Leaders*, Supplements to Novum Testamentum 51 (Leiden: E. J. Brill, 1978); Adele Reinhartz, *The Word in the World: The Cosmological Tale in the Fourth Gospel* (Atlanta, Ga.: Scholars Press, 1992); Jonathan D. Brumberg-Kraus, "Symposium Scenes in Luke's Gospel with Special Attention to the Last Supper," Ph.D. diss., Vanderbilt University (Ann Arbor, Mich.: UMI, 1991).

13. M. Eugene Boring, *The Continuing Voice of Jesus: Christian Prophecy and the Gospel Tradition* (Louisville, Ky.: Westminster/John Knox Press, 1991), 138.

14. Ibid., 138 (emphasis mine).

15. Jacob Neusner and Bruce D. Chilton, *Revelation: The Torah and the Bible*, Christianity and Judaism: The Formative Categories (Valley Forge, Pa.: Trinity Press International, 1995), xii (emphasis mine).

16. David Novak, *Jewish-Christian Dialogue: A Jewish Justification* (New York: N.Y.: Oxford University Press, 1989), 86. Novak says, "The Law—Halakhah—[is] the indispensible norm of the Jewish relationship with God" as Jesus in his "role as the Christ [is] the indispensible norm of the Christian relationship with God." See also Brumberg-Kraus, "Jewish Ideological Perspective," 136, 151.

17. Jonathan Brumberg-Kraus, "'Not by Bread Alone. . .:' The Ritualization of Food and Table Talk in the Passover Seder and in the Last Supper," *Semeia* (forthcoming).

18. Ironically, this can also mean that the central symbols of Judaism are as religiously insignificant to some assimilated Jews as Jesus is to some secularized Christians. Gift-giving supplants lighting the menorah as the central rite of Chanukah in a secularized Christian culture that has transformed the religious event of the birth of Jesus into an orgy of consumerism.

19. Jacob Neusner, *The Way of Torah*, 4th ed. (Belmont, Calif.: Wadsworth, 1988), 29. See my discussion in Brumberg-Kraus, "Jewish Ideological Perspective," 129–30.

20. Donald Hagner, *The Jewish Reclamation of Jesus: An Analysis of the Modern Jewish Study of Jesus* (Grand Rapids: Wm. B. Eerdmans Publishing Co., 1984).

21. Brumberg-Kraus, "Jewish Ideological Perspective," 128–29, 131.

22. Samuel Sandmel, *Anti-Semitism in the New Testament?* (Philadelphia: Fortress Press, 1978).

23. Brumberg-Kraus, "Jewish Ideological Perspective," 125–6.

24. Jacob Neusner, *From Politics to Piety: The Emergence of Pharisaic Judaism* (New York: N.Y.: KTAV 1978), 67: "[New Testament scholarship] routinely addresses its problems to rabbinic literature, making use of sayings and stories in that literature

concerning the life of Jesus and the history of the early church. We now reverse the question: What can be learned from the New Testament in the study of Pharisaism?" See my discussion of the ideological significance of this and similar Jewish positions in Brumberg-Kraus, "Jewish Ideological Perspective," 129–30, 147, note 50.

25. Brumberg-Kraus, "Jewish Ideological Perspective," 135.

26. Benjamin Harshav, *The Meaning of Yiddish* (Berkeley, Calif.: University of California Press, 1990), 122.

27. Brumberg-Kraus, "Jewish Ideological Perspective," 134. The quotations are from Harshav, *Meaning of Yiddish*, 122.

28. Ibid., 133.

29. Ibid. Sarah Tanzer is Jewish, and the associate professor of Judaism and Christian Origins at McCormick Theological Seminary in Chicago.

30. Ibid., 135–39.

31. Obviously, those chosen few who have had precisely those kinds of charismatic experiences of Christ in their lives would disagree vehemently with this assessment. Christians from evangelical backgrounds who take my classes constantly remind me that their experiences of the Holy Spirit give them a very different perspective on the nature of Christ from mine. Nor does it escape my notice that these same Christian students probably view my pursuit of the study of Christian scripture as an example of the power of the "Living Christ" to influence even nonbelievers! So it is precisely the convincing witness of their own charismatic experiences that has shaped my emphasis on "*other people's* religious experience" in my definition of Jesus. Nevertheless, I also find that many of my Christian academic colleagues are more comfortable with the view of Jesus as "text" to be interpreted than with evangelical views of Christ as a charismatic experience. I owe these insights to my conversations with my students Takeyla Brothers and Deshawnda Williams.

32. As had been the case before, according to Rosemary Radford Ruether's forceful statement in her critique of Christian anti-Semitism, *Faith and Fratricide: The Theological Roots of Anti-Semitism* (New York: Seabury Press, 1974), 246: "Is it possible to say 'Jesus is Messiah' without, implicitly or explicitly, saying at the same time 'and the Jews be damned'?"

33. Graham, "Scripture," 134, 141.

34. Edward Schillebeeckx, *Jesus : An Experiment In Christology*, trans. Hubert Hoskins (New York : Seabury Press, 1979). See, for example, this statement on page 58:

> Neither Jesus nor the earliest church community constitutes the origin and fount of Christianity, but *both together as offer and response. . . .* This source event, the fashioning of the Christian congregation, does indeed have its normative value: *the Jesus event in its effect on a group of people. Constantly repeated contact with the primary response to an initial offer remains normative*, therefore, for its own response [my emphasis].

35. Paul M. Van Buren, *A Theology of the Jewish Christian Reality* (New York: Seabury Press, 1980, vols. 1–2), (San Francisco: Harper Row, 1980, vol. 3); Elisabeth Schüssler Fiorenza, *In Memory of Her: A Feminist Theological Reconstruction of Christian Origins* (New York: Crossroad, 1983), esp. 106–10.

# EPILOGUE

*Leonard J. Greenspoon*

Jesus the Jew—if there is one concept in contemporary historical Jesus research ready-made for fruitful Jewish-Christian dialogue, surely this is it. We need look no further than the papers collected in this volume for scholarly confirmation.

What I wish to reflect upon here has to do with interfaith dialogue at the "popular" level. My reflections are based primarily on my own experience and that of my colleagues during the planning, organization, and implementation of the two colloquia described by Father Hamm in his introduction. He has chronicled the origins and scope of these events from the perspective of the scholars involved and the intellectual/ theological issues raised. I want to shift the focus to the audience, actual and intended. By their nature, my remarks are more impressionistic and less susceptible to quantification. But, I believe, they are no less significant for an overall evaluation that might distinguish "what was" from "what might have been."

At the time of the 1997 colloquium, we estimated that it drew about 275 people. I would say that number may actually be slightly low if we take into account the ebb and flow of student attendance. The colloquium took place on the Creighton campus, which is in an urban downtown location, on a Saturday. The majority of all-day attendees were from off campus, but the placement of this event on campus (plus some judicious prodding by faculty) certainly enhanced student attendance.

It is my impression that, except for myself, the audience was made up entirely of Christians. This remark on my part is in no way critical, but simply describes my recollection (and is buttressed by evaluation forms filled out by many in attendance). Given the fact that the title of

Dan Harrington's talk included the explicit wording "Jewishness of Jesus," we might have imagined that some members of Omaha's Jewish community (which numbers between six and seven thousand) would have been there. However, beginning the colloquium on a Saturday morning effectively excluded almost all potential Jewish audience members, since this is the time when all synagogues hold worship services. I myself had to shuttle back and forth between Creighton and my synagogue, no small feat given the 120 blocks that separate them. Few others, I suspect, felt inclined to make a similar trek.

As we planned the second colloquium, all of whose scholar-speakers were Jewish, we almost automatically scheduled it on a Sunday, thereby allowing our participants and potential Jewish audience members alike to observe the Sabbath. The audience for this 1998 event was no less enthusiastic and asked no fewer questions than the earlier one, but it was much smaller—by a factor of at least fifty percent. Creighton's student center was again the venue, and the format was very similar. We succeeded in attracting some individuals from Omaha's Jewish community; the number of Christians, both students and those from off campus, was far smaller, however.

The point of my relating these figures is to provide a context for my sense that somehow we missed an opportunity, an opportunity to further "grassroots" Jewish-Christian dialogue. Admittedly, this was not a major goal of the colloquia; in fact, I am not sure that we ever explicitly mentioned it. However, as I look back and sort out my own feelings, I ask myself (and through this epilogue, others) whether there were some ways in which we could have reshaped these events so they would have become a catalyst for continuing community-wide dialogue. Without in any way diminishing our achievement, or more correctly the achievement of our seven presenters, I think that there are additional factors we could have taken into account, even if we did not consistently accord them highest priority.

It would perhaps have made more sense to include both Jewish and Catholic scholars on both panels. I felt—and still feel—that it was worthwhile to offer the unparalleled opportunity for a group of Jewish scholars to discuss among themselves, at a personal as well as professional level, what it means when Jews study the New Testament. For many, a highlight of our second colloquium was the fifteen minutes allotted to each scholar, in which he or she spoke autobiographically about entering into the distinctly "un-Jewish" world of Christian origins and historical Jesus research. I don't think the intensity of these self-revelations, or of many other things that went on that Sunday, would have been possible in a different, more conventional setting.

Nonetheless, the question remains: Was this format, however "revolutionary," conducive to drawing together a substantial Jewish-Christian audience? Apparently, as the numbers demonstrate, the answer is no. Why was this so? Here I must be speculative. For many Jews, any reference to the New Testament and to Jesus, even a Jewish Jesus, is a turn-off. Too many times we have been bombarded by a "Christian" message that denigrates our faith by contrasting the eternal nature of the new covenant with the supposedly outmoded status of the old. And even though most Midwestern Jews have friendly relations with Christians and other non-Jews, they have little interest in studying Christian origins. At the institutional level, this is dramatically exemplified by the fact that one of our speakers, Michael Cook (from Hebrew Union College in Cincinnati), teaches the only required course on Christianity at any of the seminaries where rabbis are trained. In sum, holding a colloquium on Sunday is a definite plus in attracting Jews as an audience; having a panel made up entirely of Jewish scholars is, at best, a neutral point.

Would it not be especially attractive for Christians to hear a distinguished group of Jewish researchers discuss their views on the religion of Jesus? Apparently, it would not be—or at least, it was not. What scholars find absolutely fascinating does not, it turns out, always translate into something of popular interest, to say nothing of appeal. We should also not overlook the possibility, or rather probability, that Sunday's status as a family day (even when attendance at church on Saturday evening is an acceptable alternative) kept some Christians from participating.

Perhaps Christian laity are more comfortable learning about their faith from coreligionists. Even so, I am convinced that the audience for the first colloquium would have been no smaller had there been one or more Jews to complement, as it were, the Catholic speakers. Possibly, presentations by Jewish scholars could have been placed later on Saturday, alleviating some of the conflict inherent with scheduling on the Sabbath. Nonetheless, when (almost) all is said and done, it is apparent, at least to me, that there is no perfect format, no perfect venue, no perfect fit—and no "neutral" day or even time of day.

Some readers of this volume may be wondering what my problem is. The high quality, substantively as well as methodologically, of its contents may well be closely connected with the formats we established for the colloquia, with more traditional formats producing less valuable papers than those published here. But, I must admit, I want it all.

And I think we could have come closer to achieving that if we had taken a few additional steps. First, we needed to involve the Catholic and Jewish communities earlier and more fully in the planning and especially the publicizing of these events. This is not to say, of course, that we lacked publicity. But, I have come to learn, we as scholars do not always take into account the feelings of the members-at-large (as it were) in our community. Perhaps we would have learned that two panels— each containing both Jewish and Christian scholars, one scheduled on a Saturday and one on a Sunday, one on the Creighton campus and one on the campus of Omaha's Jewish Community Center—are just what the public desired. We may have learned, on the other hand, that the formats of our two colloquia were just fine, but that they needed to be "sold" with greater sensitivity to the perceptions (and even misconceptions) of various potential constituencies. It might also have been a good idea to seek cosponsorship with educational groups within the Jewish and Catholic (Christian) communities, and to involve interfaith councils and initiatives already in place. Academicians work hard, at least the academicians I know and respect. It was no simple task to do what we did, and to have done it well. Frankly, I do not know if we had the energy to have done more. But I am not one who wishes to close off options or preclude greater participation, even in retrospect.

In any case, let me close on what I hope is a reasonably and appropriately positive note. We have all, I would like to think, moved beyond an understanding of "interfaith dialogue" as a forum for proselytizing or a locus for feel-good therapy. Although not perfectly realized, our colloquia did provide opportunities for recognition of the profound values we share and for acknowledgment that there are areas in which we must respectfully agree to disagree. Jews and Christians can never arrive at a picture of Jesus on which they will fully agree. But, by working together, we can construct a fuller picture of the Jesus of history and the Jesus of faith, the Jesus who was a Jew, the Jesus acclaimed as Messiah by Christians.